THE ULTIMATE CAREER GUIDE FOR BUSINESS MAJORS

THE ULTIMATE CAREER GUIDE FOR BUSINESS MAJORS

Jamie Rizzo, CFA

ISBN: 1544059795
ISBN 13: 9781544059792
Library of Congress Control Number: 2017903484
CreateSpace Independent Publishing Platform
North Charleston, South Carolina

Edited by Graham Witherall; Illustrations by Deanna First

TABLE OF CONTENTS

ACKNOWLEDGEMENTS

I would like to express a very special thanks and my sincerest gratitude to Graham Witherall for his guidance and tireless editing work. He helped me organize my thoughts and kept me tightly focused on making this material as useful as possible for readers exploring a business career.

Additionally, I would like to thank the dozens of friends and colleagues who consulted on this project. This book covers wide career terrain and I am fortunate to have so many friends who have thrived in the positions covered. Kimberly Abend, Marc Angel, Jeannie Chon, Chris Droussiotis, Gary Feldman, Shawn Gannon, Britton Harold, Daniel Herscovici, Bennett LaGreca, Kevin Lam, Jeff Lesserson, Steve Lillis, Melissa Link, Deborah Murnin, Kevin McCaughan, Mike Mustillo, Anthony Providenti, Patrick Regan, Mike Simonton and Dennis Valentino - I consider you some of the smartest people I know and I appreciate the expertise and consultation you contributed. Readers should know these people have enjoyed successful careers as product managers, marketers, Wall Street analysts, investment bankers, and in other important roles. Today, they all have impressive business experience but at one time were, just like you, curious about which career path to pursue.

"What does everyone do in their office all day?"
–Mary Tigani Seelig (my grandmother)

INTRODUCTION

A conversation with my nephew prompted me to write this book. He was heading off to college and wanted to study business. But he had little idea of what it meant to be an analyst, an auditor, or a consultant. He and many others in his position were just like my grandmother who couldn't fathom what businesspeople actually do in their offices all day.

My goal is to remove the mystery from the business world and help you select a path that suits your personality, strengths, and interests.

During the past 20 years, my career has included many different roles. Early in my career I held positions in financial planning and analysis, treasury, and strategy. In these roles I regularly worked with product managers, accountants, and investment banking professionals. I also worked in business development, served as an executive producer on a major motion picture and helped a young technology company pitch its product to Silicon Valley venture capital firms. More recently, I have held roles as a Wall Street analyst where I analyzed hundreds of business models, managed billions of dollars, and met with chief executive, financial, and operating officers across dozens of industries.

I mention these things only to provide some insight on my business background. Cumulatively, that experience allowed me to work in, work with, or be a client of every one of the 32 professions covered in this book.

My hope is that this book will illustrate the many possibilities the business world offers and help you select your most suitable role. By understanding your business career choices you can determine which field fits you best. You may even decide that business is not the right career for you. I hope that's not the case because the business world can be dynamic, fulfilling, and rewarding. It's all about finding the right fit.

The Syllabus Test

The syllabus often served as a reliable predictor for the enjoyment I would get out of the classes I took as an undergraduate, a grad student, and while preparing for the Chartered Financial Analyst (CFA) exam. I recall reading the description of a CFA exam course and feeling genuinely excited to learn about financial statement analysis and equity derivatives. My intuition was correct and the learning was a pleasure.

I suggest you employ a similar approach with this book. Read each career section to gauge whether the material appeals to you. Compare how compelling one career seems against another. Many people spend years slogging through multiple jobs before finding one they enjoy. This book helps you shortcut that process by comparing dozens of professions in a manageable format. The examples listed throughout the book give you a feel for the actual functions of each job.

When reading this book, ask yourself which sections excite you most. You may have found your business calling.

Compensation, Stress and Other Common Items

The syllabus test will help you pick a rewarding career path and maximize your overall satisfaction. But recognize that every profession has drawbacks. Most positions have work-life balance challenges and can require long hours and cause stress. These are common elements so they are not directly addressed in each section.

Additionally, I do not discuss salaries in this book for two reasons. First, successful people across all the careers outlined earn a good living. All things being equal, you should not have money worries if you become successful in your chosen field. More importantly, finding a career that fits your personality should outweigh the compensation you receive. The personal fulfillment derived from helping a company gain market share or unearthing a high-return investment is far more rewarding, in my opinion.

The 'What' versus the 'How To'

This book delivers a birds-eye view of careers you can pursue with a business degree. When possible, I include details about the position and mention business and financial concepts required to succeed in each role.

I do not teach specific business and financial concepts here. You will not learn how to develop a successful marketing campaign or discount a series of cash flows. Your professors will teach those concepts in school as you pursue your degree.

To offer as much insight as possible, I include a set of examples to illustrate each career. The examples range from real events such as Microsoft buying LinkedIn to real-world situations with fictional characters and companies. For the latter, I use fictional companies simply denoted as "ABC Company" or "XYZ Bank". While the individuals and companies in those examples are fictional, the substance is equally relevant as they represent real situations individuals face every day in their jobs.

My sincere wish is that you'll find the career descriptions and examples to be helpful planning tools. Ultimately, I hope they prove instrumental in helping you discover a career you love.

PART I

OVERVIEW

THREE CAREER 'BUCKETS'

T he easiest way to understand the business world and to refine a career search is to categorize professions into three buckets. These buckets serve as the basis for everything discussed in the following pages. The three buckets are:

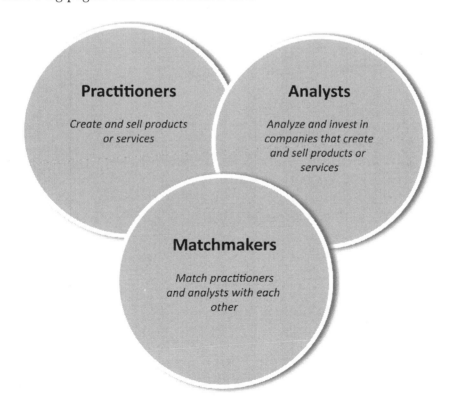

Practitioners

Create and sell products or services

Analysts

Analyze and invest in companies that create and sell products or services

Matchmakers

Match practitioners and analysts with each other

Bucket #1: Practitioners:

Think of practitioners as the "doers"—people who run the day-to-day operations of a company and steer its decision making.

Careers within this bucket include product management, sales, marketing, strategy, and business development. Operations, treasury, financial planning and analysis (FP&A), accounting, tax, and investor relations, among others also belong in the practitioner bucket.

Throughout this book you will find examples of people developing, manufacturing, marketing, distributing, financing, and selling products. Additionally, you will read examples of high-level decisions about joint ventures and mergers and acquisitions that boost a company's profile or increase sales opportunities.

Employers within the practitioners bucket include any and every company you can think of—each has their own set of practitioners! The examples provided throughout the practitioners section will give you a good understanding of the variety of companies you could work for one day.

Bucket #2: Analysts:

Careers in the analysts bucket take an outsider's view of a company and decide whether or not to invest in or lend to a company. They base their decisions on valuations and business prospects. An analyst had to decide whether to invest in Kodak just as the world of photography was about to completely change. Once Kodak's fortunes began sliding, analysts had to determine whether to hold a Kodak investment or sell it for pennies on the dollar.

The specific careers within this bucket include buy-side investors, hedge-fund analysts, private-equity analysts, commercial bankers, and sell-side analysts, to name a few.

Naturally, the lines around each profession can blur. All practitioners use a high degree of analysis in their work. As such, this second bucket could just as well be called "Outside Analysts" or "External Analysts" given the outsiders viewpoint. To keep things as simple as possible, we refer to this second bucket simply as "Analysts" since it is a handy general description of a group of specific jobs that is well known across the financial community.

Employers within the analysts bucket predominantly include asset managers, banks, and other financial services firms.

Bucket #3: Matchmakers:

The third bucket is comprised of people who match corporations with investors, corporations with other corporations, and investors with other investors. Their goal is to advise companies and investors on the capital markets and general business environment. Matchmakers collect fees for transactions such as mergers, acquisitions, or the sale of a stock or bond.

The specific careers within this bucket include the entire investment-banking world along with various subcategories of trading and financial sales.

Like the analyst role, employers in the matchmakers bucket include asset managers, banks, and other financial services firms.

What Jobs Fits in Each Bucket?

My approach to discussions about practitioners is different from how I treat analysts and matchmakers. I use departments to delve into practitioners given the variety and depth of the careers found here. Marketing, for example, is a very general term for a career with many layers and career progressions. I use job titles for analysts and matchmakers since they typically reside in "flatter" organizations where entry-level employees perform similar work to more senior people.

With our three categories in mind, here is how I categorize the careers discussed in this book:

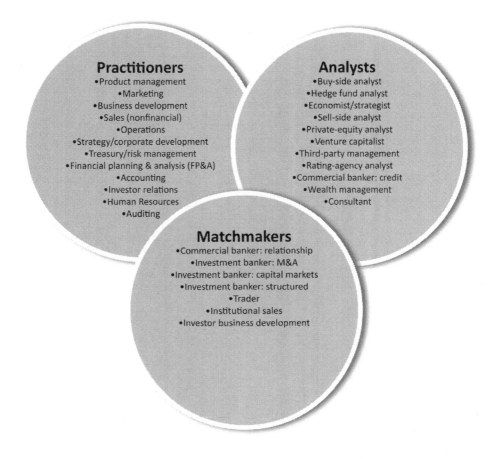

Practitioners
- Product management
- Marketing
- Business development
- Sales (nonfinancial)
- Operations
- Strategy/corporate development
- Treasury/risk management
- Financial planning & analysis (FP&A)
- Accounting
- Investor relations
- Human Resources
- Auditing

Analysts
- Buy-side analyst
- Hedge fund analyst
- Economist/strategist
- Sell-side analyst
- Private-equity analyst
- Venture capitalist
- Third-party management
- Rating-agency analyst
- Commercial banker: credit
- Wealth management
- Consultant

Matchmakers
- Commercial banker: relationship
- Investment banker: M&A
- Investment banker: capital markets
- Investment banker: structured
- Trader
- Institutional sales
- Investor business development

What is the Career for You?

The chart below includes some general characteristics often found within each career bucket. Consider these as a starting point as you begin determining what kind of work environment you desire and where your personality may best fit.

This is a very general summary. There are nuances in each role and some roles require exceptions to these generalizations. Use this chart to begin refining your search. More specific details about each position are in the pages ahead.

General Characteristics

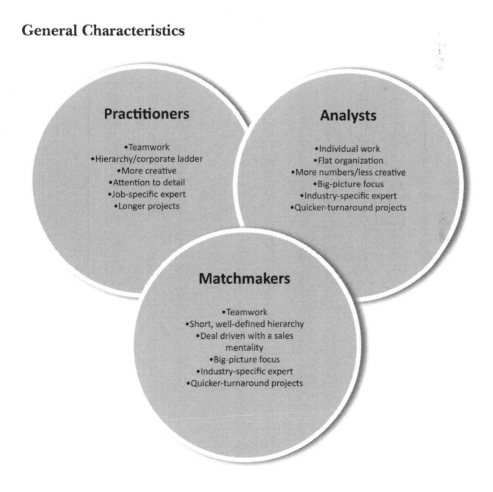

Practitioners
- Teamwork
- Hierarchy/corporate ladder
- More creative
- Attention to detail
- Job-specific expert
- Longer projects

Analysts
- Individual work
- Flat organization
- More numbers/less creative
- Big-picture focus
- Industry-specific expert
- Quicker-turnaround projects

Matchmakers
- Teamwork
- Short, well-defined hierarchy
- Deal driven with a sales mentality
- Big-picture focus
- Industry-specific expert
- Quicker-turnaround projects

Seven Important Questions

When considering a business career, people have many questions about professions. This book answers seven important questions that consistently arise when people explore careers:

(1) What are the job's day-to-day functions? In other words, what will I do?
(2) What skills and qualities help with this career?
(3) Where can this career lead?
(4) Is teamwork important in this career?
(5) What personality type thrives in this career?
(6) What's the best undergraduate major for this career?
(7) Is there a graduate degree or professional certification that helps with this career?

Question 1: What will I do?

Question 2: What skills and qualities help with this career?

These two questions lay the foundation for every career section in this book. You will find a general overview of each career and bullet lists detailing the important attributes to succeed. You will also see real-world examples of tasks people working in these careers regularly tackle.

Question 3: Where can this career lead?

It helps to know where a journey may lead before taking the first step. Most career paths take twists and turns. Many people change careers, get sidetracked, or step off the career ladder along the way. But it remains important to know what the top of the ladder looks like.

Here are the four ultimate career destinations used in this book:

(1) Chief Executive Officer (CEO)
(2) Chief Financial Officer (CFO)
(3) Chief Investment Officer (CIO)
(4) Managing Director or Partner.

Some extremely important lieutenant roles lie just below these four positions, including chief marketing officer (CMO), chief operating officer (COO), chief accounting officer (CAO), and the various general/product/portfolio managers we discuss in this book. In fact, consider the cover of this book. The roads to CEO, CFO, CIO and Managing Director / Partner could have signs all along the roadway with these lieutenant roles. In fact, careers that lead to these lieutenant roles are the crux of this book.

It is important to have a good understanding of the top four positions, how people land there, and how the four roles differ.

Path #1: Chief Executive Officer

CEOs typically rise via a practitioner career path. The CEO is responsible for leading an organization, developing a strategy that keeps a company innovative, overseeing all operations, and motivating employees. The CEO needs a sales mentality and must be a proponent of a company's products. All functions under "Product Management," "Marketing,"

"Business Development", "Operations" and "Sales" in the pages ahead are the ultimate responsibility of the CEO.

Path: CEO	
Prerequisite Career:	Bucket:
Product management	Practitioner
Marketing	Practitioner
Business development	Practitioner
Sales	Practitioner
Strategy / corporate development	Practitioner
Operations	Practitioner

This is how some high-profile CEOs cultivated their skills:

- Disney CEO Bob Iger got his start in *operational* capacities for the company's TV group.
- IBM CEO Virginia Rometty previously held positions in *product management, operations, sales,* and *strategy.*
- Apple CEO Tim Cook served as an *operations* executive, responsible for establishing the company's world-class global supply chain and manufacturing processes.
- Xerox CEO Ursula Burns worked in *product management* early in her career.
- Cisco CEO Chuck Robbins started as an account manager and rose through the *sales* and *business development* ranks for 18 years before being named CEO.

This book does not include a specific section on entrepreneurship but it runs through many of the roles explored in these pages. With that in mind, entrepreneurs should focus on the roles that lead to the CEO career path to prepare for their futures.

Path #2: Chief Financial Officer

The CFO is responsible for all things financial: budgeting, mergers and acquisitions, projecting, cost cutting, raising capital, cash management, and tax planning. A CFO also oversees financial statements, deals with auditors, meets with investors, and is a partner to the CEO on corporate startegy.

The CFO role is typically achieved via the practitioners' career path. The CFO reports directly to the CEO and the board of directors. While not always required, it is wise for people who aspire to the CFO role to at least earn a minor in accounting.

Path: CFO	
Prerequisite Career:	Bucket:
Strategy / corporate development	Practitioner
Treasury	Practitioner
Financial planning & analysis (FP&A)	Practitioner
Corporate accounting	Practitioner
Investor relations	Practitioner
Auditor	Practitioner

Here is how some CFOs earned their positions:

- Expedia CFO Mark Okerstrom served in the company's *strategy* unit at a time when it spent over $600 million on acquisitions to expand the company's global footprint.
- MSCI CFO Kathleen Winters held *financial planning and analysis* and *accounting* positions at Honeywell, including as CFO of its performance-materials business unit.
- United Rentals CFO William Plummer was previously *treasurer* of Alcoa.

Path #3: Chief Investment Officer

The CIO role is typically achieved via the analyst bucket. The CIO is ultimately responsible for preserving capital and generating returns. A CIO oversees all investment decisions: how assests are allocated between equities, bonds, and real estate and how those assets perform. Many CIOs have served as a portfolio manager before assuming the investment officer position.

Be aware that the acronym CIO can also be used as an acronym for a Chief Information Officer, which refers to someone within the technology department. This is a completely different career that falls outside the scope of this book.

Path: CIO	
Prerequisite Career:	Bucket:
Buy-side investor	Analyst
Hedge-fund analyst	Analyst
Economist / strategist (buy-side)	Analyst
Third-party manager	Analyst
Commercial banker: credit officer	Analyst
Trader	Matchmaker

Path #4: Managing Director / Partner

The fourth road, managing director or partner, covers titles for people who reach the top of their field in various sectors, such as financial services. These people are company leaders and often become part owners in their firms. This road usually draws from buckets #2 and #3: analysts and matchmakers.

Path: Managing Director / Partner	
Prerequisite Career:	Bucket:
Auditor	Practitioner
Economist / strategist (sell-side)	Analyst
Private-equity analyst	Analyst
Venture capitalist	Analyst
Sell-side analyst	Analyst
Rating agency analyst	Analyst
Wealth manager	Analyst
Consultant	Analyst
Commercial banker: relationship manager	Matchmaker
Investment banker	Matchmaker
Trader / Institutional sales	Matchmaker
Investor business development	Matchmaker

Question #4: Is teamwork important in this career?

Some people thrive as team players while others prefer an individual approach. Collaborating with others is important but the level of teamwork varies depending on your job. To help you select a suitable position, each career in this book is assigned a level for the importance of teamwork: high, medium, or low. Before labeling yourself a team player or a solo practitioner, keep in mind some pros and cons of each. A high level of teamwork may be preferable for someone that enjoys being part of team accomplishments, while a low level of teamwork may be preferable for someone that prefers to work alone. The downside to high teamwork could include a less nimble work environment and the need to deal with a greater variety of personalities and work ethics. The downside to low teamwork could include fewer subjective goals.

Question #5: What Personality type thrives in this career?

The fifth question addresses the personality traits usually required in each career. While there are many kinds of personalities, focus on whether you are more of an "extrovert" or "introvert." Consider the following attributes to determine where you stand on this spectrum from a business perspective.

Naturally, there is a broad spectrum of personality types and not everyone fits neatly into the introvert or extrovert category. Use this label as simply a helpful guide post in your career search. These labels are not intended as a commentary on the majority of workers in a particular field but rather how their job details shake out.

Personality	Job Attributes
Extrovert	<ul><li>Public speaking</li><li>High interaction with clients (external and internal)</li><li>Sales</li><li>Entertaining</li><li>More travel</li></ul>
Introvert	<ul><li>No or little public speaking</li><li>Low interaction with clients</li><li>No sales</li><li>No entertaining</li><li>Less travel</li></ul>

Question #6: What's the best undergraduate major?

Each career covered in this book includes common degrees people in that field have earned. Keep in mind that schools use various major titles and include different courses to achieve degrees. Don't worry if your school does not offer the exact major listed. Use the suggested majors as general indicators of avenues to specific careers.

Questions #7: What graduate degree is helpful in this field?
A beautiful thing about the business field is that you can enter it from different directions. Even if you choose a non-conventional undergraduate major, there are plenty of ways to get on the business track. A master's in business administration (MBA), a joint MBA-JD (juris doctorate, or law degree), or a master's degree in finance are all common routes.

In addition to graduate degrees, professional certifications can be extremely helpful in many careers. The Certified Public Accountant (CPA), Chartered Financial Analyst (CFA), Certified Financial Planner (CFP), Certified Treasury Professional (CTP), Financial Risk Manager (FRM) and the Chartered Alternative Investment Analyst (CAIA) are examples of common certifications. In these pages, certifications such as the CFA charter and the CPA are grouped in the advanced degree list on each career page.

The career pages in this book are dedicated to answering questions #1 and #2. But I also provide a header that lists details around questions #3 - #7. All seven questions are based on my personal experience and view of the business world. There are no scientific studies or surveys here. Many other aspects of a career could influence you more. These might include the frequency of travel, the ability to be creative, and the ability to work with numbers, to name a few. All are addressed in the coming pages.

Glossary of Terms for Career Pages

The business world is full of acronyms. Some are used for the degrees and qualifications people earn to progress in their professions. Others cover commonly used job titles. The following is a glossary of the acronyms used in the careers detailed in the pages ahead.

CAIA:	Chartered Alternative Investment Analyst
CEO:	Chief Executive Officer
CFO:	Chief Financial Officer
CIO:	Chief Investment Officer
CMO:	Chief Marketing Officer
CFA:	Chartered Financial Analyst
CFP:	Certified Financial Planner
CMA:	Certified Management Accountant
CPA:	Certified Public Accountant
CTP:	Certified Treasury Professional
FRM:	Financial Risk Manager
JD:	Juris Doctor (law degree)
LLM:	Masters of Laws
MBA:	Masters in Business Administration
MD:	Managing Director
Mgmt. Info. Systems:	Management Information Systems
MS:	Masters of Science

PART II

THE DETAIL

BUCKET #1: PRACTITIONERS

The first set of careers we'll examine are practitioners, the "doers" who typically create a company's product and run the day-to-day operations.

For the sake of clarity, think of "Bucket #1: Practitioners" in two smaller categories:

- Lead practitioners, including product managers, marketing, business development, sales, strategy, corporate development, and sometimes operations.
- Support practitioners, including financial planning and analysis, treasury, accounting, tax, investor relations, human resources, and sometimes operations.

Some careers straddle the dividing line between categories. Be aware that some roles – typically the ones considered lead practitioners who are directly responsible for generating revenue – can have a greater decision-making impact on major issues than support practitioners.

Know the Language: A Primer on Corporations, Business Units, and General Managers

Large, major companies that sell a variety of products and operate in different parts of the country or world are structured in different ways. A company could have from one to dozens of business units.

Take Johnson & Johnson, for example. It sells everything from mouthwash and Band-Aids to drugs that treat major illnesses and medical devices used in life-saving surgeries. Consumer products, pharmaceuticals, and medical devices are separate business units within the same company. These business units are also divided geographically between the United States and international markets, creating six different units. Each has its own set of practitioners in product management, marketing, sales, operations, and financial planning and analysis.

Each unit has a budget and while its finances are tied to the overall company, a business unit often has the power to make its own investments.

While Johnson & Johnson has just one Chief Executive Officer, each business unit (or geographic region) has a "CEO" of its own. These people are typically referred to as the general manager (GM). Other common terms for this role are president and executive vice president (EVP). In this book, we will refer to the role as the GM. There is not a specific section on a GM career. It is essentially a mini-CEO. That person's background is covered in the practitioner area in which the GM was trained.

Organization Chart Example

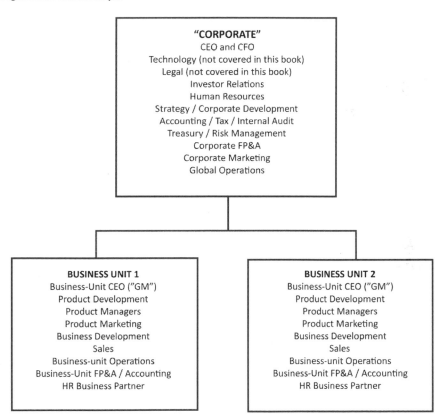

For an example of a GM's career path, consider Jim Umpleby, CEO of Caterpillar, the maker of tractors and other heavy equipment. Before being named the corporation's CEO, Umpleby had a 35-year Caterpillar career. Prior to landing the top job, he was group president of the company's energy and transportation segment, essentially the GM of one of Caterpillar's three business units. Previously, he held positions in engineering, manufacturing, sales, marketing, and customer service, including assignments in Singapore and Malaysia.

Mr. Umpleby's rise at Caterpillar illustrates the climb to CEO through the practitioner role. It's typically a culmination of many years learning the business in multiple roles. **CEOs are typically made, rather than being born to the position**.

Know the Language: Where are you in the Matrix?

Most businesses have what's known as a "matrix reporting structure." Simply put, this means that one individual can report to multiple different bosses. Consider a business-unit financial planning and analysis individual who reports to the business-unit GM on one hand and the corporate CFO on the other.

Each company builds their own unique matrix. They may also use slightly different terms for their careers, where those positions are located within the organization, and to whom those positions ultimately report. For example, a common entry-level position could be called business analyst, research analyst, or associate. These titles can be found in just about every department of an organization including marketing, sales, and product management. As you progress through your career, common titles will include assistant vice president, project manager, vice president, and director.

As you come across entry-level practitioner career opportunities, the important thing for you to take away from this section of the book is *where* the role resides within the entire company more so than the title itself.

Know the Language: What's an Industry Vertical and why does it Matter?

Before moving into the specifics for the practitioners bucket, be cognizant of the industry you want to work in. In the business world, it is common to refer to a specific industry as a "vertical."

The number of industry verticals is large: consumer products, technology, television, food, beverage, automotive, aerospace, medical products, pharmaceuticals, transportation, and financial services, to name just a few. When you choose a career, a big part of your decision should not only be which day-to-day functions will motivate you but also which industry will capture your interest.

As a rating agency analyst, one of my junior team members struggled when he would analyze technology companies. The problem was not that it was too complicated. He simply had no passion or even interest in the technology sector.

As part of a special project, we were asked to analyze a solar panel manufacturer. On a site visit to the solar panel manufacturer, the analyst was clearly enthused about the business. On his next performance review, I encouraged him to consider switching careers to work for an alternative energy company where his true interest showed. He eventually landed a sales job with a solar panel company and said it was the best decision he ever made.

The bottom line is that picking a role in a company is an important part of your career planning and so is the industry, or "vertical," where that company operates. You'll do your best work in a field you care about.

Practitioners #1, #1a, #1b, #1c:

THE "BUSINESS PEOPLE": PRODUCT MANAGEMENT - MARKETING – BUSINESS DEVELOPMENT - SALES

The next four sections discuss product management, marketing, business development, and sales professions as separate careers. Be aware that there can be overlap between these roles. In addition, these roles will interact closely with operational and finance roles and sometimes with the strategy/corporate development teams.

You will spend a lot of time in business school learning about "the P"s: product, packaging, pricing, placement, promotion, and procurement. Decisions and strategies relating to "the P's" all occur within these practitioner roles. Between them, people in product management, marketing, business development, and sales determine the meat of most businesses. They create a business strategy for how things should be sold and determine prices for products and services. They set the terms when businesses collaborate and decide how responsibilities as well as revenues and costs will be split in partnerships.

Because of the nature of their responsibilities, professionals within product management, business development, and sales are typically called the "business people." This can also be true for professionals within marketing and operations in certain situations. Entry level roles in these areas can sometimes be referred to as business analysts. Their focus is on supporting decision-makers with data and information on market and competitive trends.

The following chart shows the inter-workings among the different groups. This is an illustrative example. Every organization has its own unique structure.

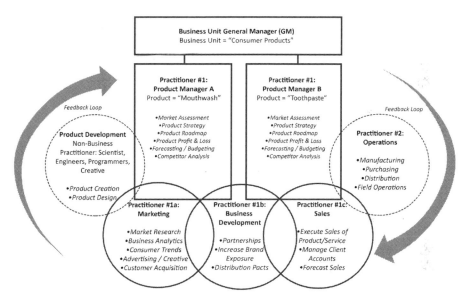

Practitioner #1

PRODUCT MANAGEMENT

Career Path	Undergraduate Degree	Advanced Degree	Personality Type	Level of Teamwork
CEO	•Marketing •Operations Mgmt •Various Sciences	MBA	Extrovert	High

Overview

Product managers are business leaders of specific products or brands. These individuals "own" a specific product or range of products and are responsible for recognizing that product's market opportunity, getting it to market, and maximizing sales. A product manager is responsible for identifying how a product will bring value to the customer and delivering on that value proposition.

The way a product is branded, marketed, and sold is called "product positioning". Product managers must determine whether their product is, for example, a discount item, clinical item, or luxury item. That determination influences sales and marketing plans.

Consider the Johnson & Johnson business unit example discussed earlier. One of the company's business units is U.S. Consumer Products. This unit includes dozens of recognizable products and brands such as Aveeno®, Neutrogena®, Rogaine®, Tylenol®, Band-Aid®, Zyrtec®, and Listerine® mouthwash. Each product or brand requires a product manager to oversee all aspects of operations and product strategy. These individuals bring the mouthwash or headache remedy to market and are responsible for the product's profitability. These individuals work closely with related business professionals in marketing, business development, finance, legal, sales, and supply chain operations.

Before diving into a product manager's day-to-day work, consider how products are created. Product development teams create, design, and test products. These individuals usually have degrees in the sciences. Product development lays the foundation for all practitioner roles. Without a product, there is no business!

To understand product development, think of the following non-business jobs:

- Engineers: Engineers design physical goods. They could be an Intel electrical engineer creating a more powerful semiconductor, a General Electric mechanical engineer designing a jet engine, or a Colgate designer crafting the latest toothpaste tube.
- Software Programmers: Programmers are the digital equivalent of product engineers. They write the code and design the end-user interface for applications, Internet sites, and database products. Consider the travel-website Expedia. The company spent three years and more than $1 billion updating its website and mobile platforms. Much of that investment went to software programmers who created a quick, powerful, and user-friendly place to book flights, hotels, rental cars, and cruises.
- Creative Professionals: The creative career spans fashion and media industries, including television, movies, sports, and news. It includes writers, producers, directors, editors, artists, and on-air talent.
- Scientists: Scientists create new medicines, consumer products, and even food.
- Data Scientists / Statisticians / Mathematicians: A fast-growing number of products use historical databases that can be sorted and analyzed for data.
- Service Professionals: In addition to creating products, practitioners also offer services. For these professionals the "product" is legal work, accounting services, architecture, and consulting to name a few.

While most people in product development are non-business personnel, the product manager role requires a business background to bridge the technical aspects of a product with the product's sales strategy. The product manager links the product development team to the sales team and ultimately to customers. Product managers help focus product development teams. In many organizations, product managers define the WHAT as they prioritize a product's features, functionality, and qualities. They also set timelines and plan deliverables. It is up to the product development team to determine the HOW as they work to create a product with the promised capabilities.

In addition to product managers, other business roles must appreciate the technical aspects of product development. Without understanding a product's technical aspects and competitive advantages it is difficult to succeed in careers related to that product. You may not be expected to design an item but you may be counted on to sell, market, or raise capital to produce it. You may also need to make prudent investment or accounting decisions based on the product.

Product Management: What will I do?

- Identify market opportunities and end-market needs
- "Own" a specific product or set of products: bring products to market, create business plans to show a market's size, highlight competitive advantages, and craft sales and distribution strategies
- Bridge product development technical experts with real-world applications and monetize those products
- Work with marketing's business analytics groups to determine pricing, consumer buying, and competitor trends and strategies
- Work with marketing's creative and advertising groups to develop compelling branding strategies and sales campaigns
- Work on design and functionality of digital products and mobile apps
- Work with finance and sales on budgets and forecast volume and pricing

- Work with marketing, operations, and sales to determine distribution strategies
- Perform "SWOT" product analysis: assess strengths, weaknesses, opportunities, and threats
- Continually assess market trends and customer feedback
- Be an expert on "omni channel" distribution: e-commerce, digital, mobile, and physical
- Identify unmet customer needs for new products, services, or product extensions
- Calculate return on investment for new product launches
- Attend trade shows to market product capabilities and to learn about competitor products and industry trends
- Manage product life-cycles and determine when to change strategic direction or to discontinue a product based on shifting consumer tastes or profitability outlook
- Work with product development, operations, corporate development, business development, and finance on "build versus buy versus partner" strategies— in other words, determine whether it's most cost effective to internally build it, acquire it from someone else, or partner with an existing provider
- Work with supply chain operations on purchasing and procurement decisions

Product Management: What skills and qualities help?

- A sales and marketing mentality
- Ability to coordinate many different groups which may not have identical priorities
- Ability to synthesize information from different sources, assess issues clearly, and make strategic decisions
- Results oriented – comfortable setting profit targets and being held accountable
- Willing to travel frequently
- Creative
- Problem solver

- Understand at least the basics of engineering, programming, and other technical areas. This is even more crucial for technology-related products
- Ability to prioritize—enjoy working under tight deadlines and achieving milestones
- Good financial acumen for pricing, margins, and profitability

Product Management Examples

- Product managers are responsible for product budgets and projections. Jacob is a packaged foods product manager. He is responsible for the company's granola bars. Each year, he provides his CEO a 12-month budget that projects monthly sales volumes, average pricing, and associated costs. This year, the budget includes Jacob's expectations for retaining 95% of existing accounts at physical retailers. He expects to lose 5% due to store closures. Jacob also projects a 3% increase in prices at retained accounts, as well as a 10% increase in new sales to online customers. Together, this results in a revenue increase of 8% while Jacob projects a 3% increase in expenses. Jacob, his team and sales meet each month to review sales results, address budget variances, and study customer feedback regarding pricing and product quality.
- Product managers are responsible for developing premium subscription tiers. CNBC.com offers a "Pro" subscription tier that includes live streaming videos, extended interviews with top asset managers, bonus video segments, and a daily email to your inbox with the day's highlights. The subscription costs $29.99/month or an annual $299.99 fee. The network offers a free 30-day trial. Product managers at CNBC are responsible for establishing the design and functionality of the site as well as the type of content to deliver free to CNBC.com versus the content that stays behind the pay wall. Marketing will typically set the subscription prices and promotion details such as optimal free-trial periods.

- Product managers look for brand extension opportunities. Consumer products company Burt's Bees is best known for its all-natural lip balms. The company has developed a loyal customer base and built a presence with pharmacies and retailers over several decades. Recognizing a consumer desire for natural products, Burt's Bees launched a line of cosmetics that leverage its reputation for quality and all-natural ingredients. The new product line includes lipsticks, eye shadow, and blush.

- Product managers are responsible for monitoring market and competitor trends. Nicole is an associate product manager for a cosmetics company. Her boss is responsible for the company's lotions, mascara, and lipstick product lines. Nicole researches market and competitor data. This includes maintaining a database of monthly pricing trends, discounting events, and product penetration at the largest retailers. Nicole's research is segmented between physical stores and e-commerce. Nicole and her colleagues visit stores to examine product placement and to see whether retailers offer promotions or favorable shelf positions for specific products.

- Product managers change a brand's image to accommodate consumer sentiment shifts. Axe® body spray entered the male-grooming market by humorously exaggerating the product's success in attracting the opposite sex. This image became dated and critics called the marketing campaigns offensive. Axe's product manager worked with its advertising agency to re-brand the product to one that celebrates the unique personalities of its customers.

- Product managers must spot changes in consumer tastes. In response to customer concerns about artificial and genetically modified ingredients, Heinz scientists and engineers created organic ketchup that eliminated ingredients such as high-fructose corn syrup.

- Many start-up companies have developed a new product manager role called "chief revenue officer." This role partners with the CEO and product developers to craft a strategy to maximize a product's profitability. This may include determining a market's size and how the sales force will attract customers. It also includes creating a revenue model: Does the company charge a recurring subscription fee? Is it a one-time transaction? Can it be both? Do you initially sell the product at a loss to earn higher-margin sales on the back end the way a razor is sold at a loss with the intention of making a profit on future razor blade sales?

- Successful product development relies on innovation. Apple engineers created the iPod and subsequently the iPhone to overtake and replace products made by competitors such as Sony's Walkman and CD Discman. Innovation creates new opportunities and expands an addressable market. A generation ago, it was unthinkable that a phone would be a camera, a GPS device, a bank, and so much more!

Practitioner #1a

MARKETING

Career Path	Undergraduate Degree	Advanced Degree	Personality Type	Level of Teamwork
•CMO •MD/Partner •CEO	•Marketing •Business Analytics	MBA	Extrovert	High

Overview

Marketing casts a wide career net. Marketers focus on customer acquisition strategies, advertising campaigns, and product positioning, all with the goal of creating demand and being top-of-mind for consumers. The marketing role is responsible for the deep-dive data analysis around customer trends. This helps establish pricing and promotional offers. Marketers are also responsible for discovering and correcting sales shortcomings. For example, are poor sales a result of limited consumer awareness? If so, marketers might recommend changes to advertising or distribution strategies. Are consumers aware of the brand but not convinced of its quality? If so, marketers may expand product trials so consumers have a better appreciation for its quality.

The varied responsibilities require a company's marketing group to work closely with product management, business development, sales, and potentially the operations and supply chain groups.

Given the breadth of marketing, consider the career in seven areas outlined below. These categories don't break neatly and there is typically some overlap. Use these categories as a guideline to consider when thinking about a marketing career. Think where you might fit best to start your career. As you advance, you will be expected to understand all these areas. An accomplished chief marketing officer (CMO) has working knowledge of each discipline:

a) <u>Advertising / Creative</u>: This role illustrates a product's value and its competitive advantages. The advertising function collaborates with product managers to determine how a product is superior to the competition and to create a strategy to tell that story. This can be achieved through traditional media advertising, in-store displays, viral campaigns, "influencer" campaigns, sponsorships, or through product placement on television shows, movies, and online media. This role works closely with the creative world—film production, graphic arts, and digital media.

b) <u>Direct Marketing / Customer Acquisition</u>: The marketing team is responsible for building brand loyalty and being top-of-mind for consumers. Customer acquisition includes developing and executing a communications strategy through traditional or social media, customized promotions, rewards programs, and other campaigns. These efforts generate sales from existing and new customers. Marketers also investigate why customers reject a brand or become "dormant" customers (people who once bought a product but have not done so recently). Customer acquisition marketing is a fascinating area that focuses on sales and monetization but also seeks insights about what motivates customers, including pricing, service, features, benefits, and perceived quality. A company's digital strategy also falls within customer acquisition and focuses on search engine optimization (making sure that your product or brand shows up when internet users search specific keywords), social media harmonization, mobile applications, and strategy development for display ads and paid search ads.

c) <u>Distribution Strategy</u>: Marketing can also establish a product's distribution strategy and maximize its "reach" for a target market. Distribution strategy has become increasingly important in e-commerce as marketing and product management teams assess the best strategy to get products from a factory to the consumer.

For consumer products, this could include selling directly to an end customer rather than selling to a traditional brick-and-mortar retailer. Distribution overlaps with the operations supply chain group that ultimately executes the strategy.

d) <u>Market Research / Data Analytics / Business Intelligence</u>: Marketing conducts research and analyzes trends to assess consumer preferences and competitor strategies. This work includes creating and administering focus groups, analyzing large banks of data, and identifying consumer buying habits that impact a product's success. This data is useful for helping establish a product strategy and brand image. The use of "Big Data" – the wealth of information about consumers accumulated through digital channels is becoming increasingly prevalent in marketing. Understanding this data can lead to wiser decisions about where to allocate limited sales and marketing resources.

e) <u>Media Planning</u>: Marketing relies on budget support to promote product awareness. Once funds are allocated, a media planner decides how best to direct the money. Typical decisions revolve around whether to spend on traditional media such as television and radio or for online viral campaigns. Selecting appropriate marketing outlets requires a marketing manager to assess the most profitable return on investment (ROI), a common method for measuring a campaign's success. ROI calculations can be complicated but the concept is simple: What is the return (usually measured in incremental profits) divided by the investment (usually the cost of a campaign / program). If a Facebook advertisement cost $100,000, for example, and it generated $500,000 worth of incremental profits, the ROI would be 500% ($500,000 / $100,000).

f) <u>Product Pricing</u>: Pricing strategy receives input from product management, sales, and marketing. Pricing research and analysis overlaps with the market research and data analytics section discussed above. It deserves a separate category since it can be extremely detailed and segmented. This includes analysis covering how to set different prices in different geographic markets, when to bundle products, and when to offer discounts. Proper pricing plays a huge role in a product's success.

g) <u>Public Relations</u>: This area typically falls outside the scope of a business degree and is more suited for a communications degree. It is an important area to keep in mind though given the tight relationship between a product's marketing strategy and the communication that accompanies those goals.

Much of the planning and execution for advertising, media planning and some other functions is performed via third-party agencies such as Omnicom, Interpublic, and WPP and their subsidiaries. The top of the career path at these third-party agencies is a Managing Director / Partner role. Careers at these third-party agencies could just as easily be included in the consulting section later in this book. The top role for in-house marketing professionals is Chief Marketing Officer. It is possible for in-house marketing professionals to rise to the CEO level although that is not a common progression.

Marketing: What will I do?

- Analyze customer trends, pricing policies, competitor practices, retail trends, promotional activities and distribution strategies
- Learn about consumers by conducting focus groups and market-research analysis to understand relevant trends and to better understand competing products. Analyze and interpret that data to determine market advantages
- Develop strategies and tactics to elevate brand awareness
- Build brand loyalty through rewards programs and targeted promotional campaigns
- Provide expertise on traditional advertising strategies such as online, television, outdoor billboard, radio, sponsorships, and product placements
- Provide expertise on digital advertising strategies related to paid-search, search engine optimization, social media, ad networks, display ads, and viral campaigns
- Work with public relations to generate favorable media coverage
- Be an expert on "omni channel" distribution: e-commerce, digital, mobile, and physical

- Develop mobile app designs and functionality
- Oversee third-party advertising agencies (for in-house marketing)
- Develop creative advertising campaigns

Marketing: What skills and qualities help?

- Creativity
- Interest in media, social media, current events, and consumer trends
- Interest in media consumption patterns such as television viewing habits or internet use
- Comfortable with technology as many of the marketing outlets, strategies, and data aggregation processes become increasingly digital, online, and automated
- Enjoy public speaking and presenting
- Analytically curious: enjoy accumulating swaths of data, mining the data, and developing data-based conclusions
- Problem solver
- Sales mentality

Marketing Examples

- Marketers help product managers make key decisions about product selection and pricing. After weeks of conducting market research via focus groups and in-store interviews, the marketing department of Company A determined it couldn't raise the price of its popular condiment because customer feedback revealed that consumers would switch to a cheaper competitor if prices rose.

  Company A's marketing department, however, determined it would be able to raise the price of its condiment brand by 20% if it switched to organic ingredients. The marketing department worked with their colleagues in the operations supply chain group to determine the cost difference between current ingredients and organic replacements to determine whether the switch was financially feasible.

- Marketing officials find product placement opportunities to position their brands. In *Orange is the New Black,* a corrections officer bribes inmates with a box of Dunkin Donuts. Audi automobiles have been shrewdly placed in action-hero movies such as *Iron Man, The Avengers,* and *Captain America.* Marketers negotiate with film production professionals on the cost and visibility of placement. This marketing approach may appear more authentic than traditional promotions because it can subtly associate known and admired characters with products in their on-air environments.

- Marketers seek sponsorship opportunities that will resonate with their desired audience. Think of college football's the FedEx Orange Bowl or ESPN's "Game Day Built by The Home Depot." Both were creations of marketing and business development officials on both sides of the equation.

- Rewards programs can be a key part of a company's marketing and customer-retention strategy. Marriott hotels licenses 13 credit card programs under the Marriott Rewards and Starwood Preferred Guest loyalty programs where card usage creates loyalty to their brands. These programs are designed to yield repeat guest business by rewarding frequent stays with points for free hotel stays and airline miles. The company believes its loyalty programs generate substantial repeat business that might otherwise go to competing hotels.

- Marketing professionals adjust to changing consumer buying habits. Cereal and snack food company Kellogg's announced a shift in distribution strategy for certain products. It will exit its Direct Store Delivery (DSD) network in favor of a warehouse model that ships products to central warehouses owned by customers. The shift was due to its customers increasingly sophisticated technology that manages inventory as consumers increasingly shop online and in a wider variety of retail locations. The new model is designed to reduce complexity and costs while driving growth and profitability. Kellogg's planned to reinvest savings into brand building and marketing initiatives.

- Marketers must keep companies current with consumer tastes. Major automakers assemble focus groups of consumers to provide feedback about vehicle design, features, and colors. Marketers from the companies analyze the data to provide feedback to their engineers and designers about what consumers like and dislike. They also share their findings with their advertising team to find advantages to highlight.

- Marketers look for opportunities to project the desired company image. Comcast frequently sponsors ReCode's annual Code Conference, which features some of technology's top leaders. Reasons for such sponsorships typically revolve around brand awareness in relation to a specific industry or demographic. In other words, Comcast recognized the value in its brand being associated with Silicon Valley's innovative technology companies.

- Customer acquisition strategies can be found all around your home. Think of all of the credit card offers or clothing catalogs you or your parents have probably received in the mail over the years. These are all crafted by a company's marketing department in an effort to increase brand awareness and capture new customers or increase the spending of existing customers (sometimes called "share of wallet"). This is also extended to the offers you may receive in your email inbox.

- Customer acquisition strategists must keep up-to-date with the latest predictive technologies. Homebuilders, for example, use technologies that help them market to first-time home buyers, months or even years before a person is looking to buy a home! These technologies target individuals doing web-searches for engagement rings, wedding dresses, and baby cribs, all activities that could be a precursor to a first-time home purchase.

- Media planners must be comfortable recommending an advertising strategy that will generate the best return on investment for a product. Natalie is a media planner for a large advertising agency. Her client is a major snack food company. Each year, Natalie allocates the client's $20 million advertising budget between television ads, internet display ads, and sponsorships. She makes her recommendations by tirelessly keeping up to date with media consumption patterns within the age 18-34 demographic, the key target market for her client.

Practitioner #1b

BUSINESS DEVELOPMENT

Career Path	Undergraduate Degree	Advanced Degree	Personality Type	Level of Teamwork
CEO	•Marketing •Strategy •Finance •Economics	•MBA •MBA-JD	Extrovert	Medium

Overview:

The business-development role draws on both marketing and sales. Think of business development in the context of a sales role that looks for new opportunities for a company. A professional in this field seeks ways to help a company grow profitably. This might be by developing new partnerships or collaborations or through discovering opportunities such as content and distribution deals.

Business Development: What will I do?

- Grow a business by increasing exposure, scale, and revenue opportunities. This could be through joint ventures, partnerships, brand licenses, or new distribution alliances
- Negotiate strategic partnerships and revenue-sharing deals
- Develop "win-win" strategies between two or more entities
- Negotiate content and distribution deals
- Focus on return on investment (ROI) whether in financial terms or brand exposure

Business Development: What skills and qualities help?

- Enjoy negotiating and closing deals
- Creativity to find avenues that increase product exposure

- Sales mentality
- Enjoy travel
- Enjoy public speaking

Business Development Examples

- Business development professionals look for strategic part-nerships around products and production. The business development team at Dunkin' Donuts helped launch a brand of ready-to-drink iced coffee beverages in a joint venture with Coca-Cola Company. Coca Cola announced that it would manufacture, distribute, and sell the product through its network of bottling partners. The drinks are sold in grocery stores, convenience stores, and Dunkin' Donuts locations. The move opened a new market for Dunkin' Donuts while avoiding the more expensive and riskier option of building its own bottling and distribution capabilities.
- Business development professionals find appropriate partners for their company. Credit card business development professionals create partnerships with hotel companies, airlines, universities, and sports leagues to deliver more customers and grow sales. These types of agreements require a strong understanding of return on investment (ROI) concepts and financial sensitivity analysis.
- Brand licensing is an important part of business development. Consider the company Entenmann's, a leading producer of baked goods such as cakes, pies and donuts. The company licenses its Entenmann's brand name for the use in scented candles manufactured by Jay Companies. The candles are scented to match iconic Entenmann's baked goods including Apple Strudel, Cinnamon Crumb Cake, and Lemon Pound Cake.
- Business development teams look for avenues to collaborate with other companies in mutually beneficial ways. Retailer Best Buy entered into agreements with Apple, Samsung, Microsoft, and others for their "store-within-a-store" concept. Business

development professionals from all companies involved negotiated how those stores would be established and how they would operate within Best Buy.

- The entertainment industry is filled with partnerships and licenses created by business development departments. Movie studio Paramount Pictures and toy company Hasbro announced a deal to collaborate on feature films for five of Hasbro's properties. Under the agreement, Paramount would feature characters from Hasbro brands, including G.I. Joe, Micronauts, Visionaries, Mobile Armored Strike Kommand, and ROM.

- Business development professionals find ways to expand the footprint and distribution of a product or service. Cable-TV Company Discovery Communications owns dozens of TV channels such as Discovery, TLC, and Animal Planet. During a five year period, the business development team increased the number of international countries its channels were broadcast in to 220 from 170 by signing new distribution pacts with local cable and satellite companies.

- Business development teams find creative ways to expand a brand's presence. FedEx announced a partnership with drugstore chain Walgreens. The alliance established FedEx drop-off and pickup services at nearly 8,000 Walgreens locations across the United States. The addition of Walgreens increased the number of locations a customer could pick-up and drop-off packages, enhancing overall convenience. Upon the announcement, FedEx stated that their research concluded that customers ranked pharmacies as a preferred location for accessing their e-commerce shipments.

Practitioner #1c

SALES (NON-FINANCIAL)

Career Path	Undergraduate Degree	Advanced Degree	Personality Type	Level of Teamwork
CEO	•Marketing •Various other	MBA	Extrovert	Low

Overview

The sales role is easy to understand but challenging to perform well. Sales employees, usually known as sales reps or account managers, make initial sales with new customers and maintain long-term relationships with existing customers. This role is ultimately responsible for closing deals, keeping customers loyal, and generating revenue.

Consider the sales role in five broad subcategories:

a) <u>Physical Products</u>: Business-to-business sales of physical products. This could be soft drinks and beauty products to grocery stores, brake pads and seat belts to auto manufacturers, or seeds and fertilizer to farmers. It also includes medicines to hospitals, computers to insurance companies, and lumber to homebuilders. Almost everything you use has been sold once, twice, or more times along the way.

b) <u>Software</u>: This includes software applications and what is known as Software-as-a-Service products ("SaaS") that are delivered from the cloud. Applications offered from Salesforce.com are an example of a SaaS product.

c) <u>Services</u>: Business-to-business sales of nonfinancial services such as consulting and legal services. The sales role is crucial to firms such as Deloitte & Touche, Boston Consulting, and Accenture, among many others that provide accounting, consulting, and strategy services. All require sales staff to prospect new clients, price their services, and maintain relationships with existing clients.

d) <u>Advertising Sales</u>: Sale of advertising space or time across all types of media—television, radio, Internet, billboard, and print, among others. ESPN, for example, sells advertising time during its games and shows.

e) <u>Financial Products and Services</u>: Sales of business-to-business financial products and services are covered later in this book under "Bucket #3: Matchmakers." Consumer financial products such as credit cards are covered in marketing.

Sales employees interact with clients so are expected to generate customer feedback about the products and services they sell. This forms a "feedback loop" to the product management and marketing teams to make product improvements and to provide insight about competitors. Is the customer seeking a better product? Are competitors offering cheaper prices? Does your client want more responsive customer service? A sales pro regularly provides this market intelligence.

Sales (nonfinancial): What will I do?

- Develop expertise about the product or service provided
- Execute product and marketing plans
- Serve as the face-to-face point of contact for customers
- Provide critical feedback and market intelligence to marketing and product management
- Prospect for new clients by discovering candidates to use your products and services
- Participate in industry trade shows and conferences
- Network in person and on social media
- Visit clients and prepare proposals in response to requests for proposals (RFPs) clients create to generate a bidding process for competitive services and pricing

Sales (nonfinancial): What skills and qualities help?

- Self-starter who is motivated
- Enjoy negotiating
- Creative—always thinking of new customers that may need your product or service
- Enjoy travel
- Strong communications skills and enjoys public speaking
- Enjoy variety rather than a daily routine
- Prefer commission-based salary that can vary widely
- Ability to rebound from rejection

Sales Examples

- Sales teams constantly seek ways to create new markets. HP Inc.'s sales team signed a deal to supply computers and handheld devices to more than 25,000 Volvo employees worldwide.
- Sales and marketing professionals share their company's products with potential customers. Each year the farm-equipment industry holds an annual trade show called Farm Progress. Sales managers from Deere, Caterpillar, Syngenta, Monsanto, and other companies host booths and demonstrate their latest products.
- Sales teams build strategy to expand their customer base. Lennox International is a leading air conditioning, heating, and refrigeration equipment manufacturer. It has a sales team that focuses on large, national retailers such as Lowe's, Advance Auto Parts, Target, and Gap. Lennox supplies air conditioning and heating systems for those companies nationwide.
- Sales professionals frequently work in an international environment. Magna International is a global automotive industry component supplier. The company's products include seats, interior and exterior mirrors, and power-train and chassis parts and systems. Company sales representatives serve large automotive manufacturers, including General Motors and Ford in the United States, BMW in Germany, and Toyota in Japan.

Practitioner #2

OPERATIONS: SUPPLY CHAIN

Career Path	Undergraduate Degree	Advanced Degree	Personality Type	Level of Teamwork
CEO	•Operations Mgmt. •Mgmt. Info Systems •Marketing	•MBA •ISO certifications •Six Sigma	Introvert	High

Overview

Operations management is a very broad field and the supply chain role is one of the highest value-added positions. Think of supply chain careers within three sub-segments:

a) <u>Manufacturing</u>: Making a physical product with a focus on process improvement and yield management by improving efficiency and reducing defects.

b) <u>Procurement and Purchasing</u>: Acquiring finished products, such as clothes, food, or toys, which are then sold by a retailer or sourcing components for a physical product, such as parts needed to manufacture an automobile.

c) <u>Distribution</u>: Moving a product from a manufacturer's floor to a customer in the most efficient and cost-effective way possible.

Supply chain professionals focus on making physical products at the lowest price while meeting quality standards. This includes negotiating with vendors for inputs needed to make a product, using the most efficient manufacturing processes, and ensuring a steady flow of product even in the face of unexpected incidents such as machine failures or supplier problems.

This role has become much more global as increased production occurs in low-cost regions throughout Asia, Eastern Europe, and Latin America.

Operations/Supply Chain: What will I do?

- Forecast and purchase supplies or final products
- Manage inventory levels and monitor industry supply-demand dynamics
- Be an expert on "omni channel" distribution, both e-commerce and physical
- Negotiate product input costs, payment terms, delivery instructions, and quality of product
- Manage and oversee processes for manufacturing, purchasing, distribution, and product returns
- Determine strategies for shipping, returns, refund and cancellation policies
- Partner with sales on "channel marketing," the process of selling a product to a distributor that eventually sells it to the end user. This is typically used to reach smaller customers. Promotions and pricing are important in this channel to encourage a distributor to carry a product
- Master the concept known as "Lean Six Sigma" which involves constantly seeking improvements by making production faster, cheaper, better, and more efficient
- Manage vendor relationships by understanding their production and delivery capabilities
- Determine global manufacturing locations by considering cost and availability of labor, ease of distribution, and proximity to end customers
- Perform in-house manufacturing versus outsourcing calculations. For example, a computer maker considers the cost of production, assembly, and delivery in a domestic plant compared to sourcing and assembling components overseas
- Be knowledgeable and current on technologies that help automate production processes, such as 3-D printing, and link a global supply-chain footprint
- Understand the credit worthiness of suppliers and customers

Operations/Supply Chain: What skills and qualities help?

- A "roll up your sleeves" work ethic
- Cost conscious personality to seek costs savings
- Awareness of the latest automation processes and trends
- Problem solver
- Desire to work on a national or global scale
- Enjoy negotiating
- Calm in crisis situations
- Enjoy managing groups focused on process execution
- An analytical approach to discover the most efficient solutions

Operations Supply Chain Examples

- Supply chain professionals consider many factors in sourcing decisions. Spanish retailer Zara is one of the most innovative supply-chain merchandisers in the retail-fashion industry. It outsources only a portion of its manufacturing to lower-cost producers in countries such as China. The majority of its suppliers' factories are located near its European headquarters. This provides greater flexibility and quicker turnarounds for fast-changing fashion trends.

    Most apparel retailers commit and manufacture nearly 80% of inventory prior to a fashion season, according to a Columbia Business School case study. In contrast, Zara commits to only 50–60% of its line at the start of the season. This gives the company the flexibility to design and manufacture a large portion of its product later, allowing it to react quickly to the popularity of styles and colors. This manufacturing approach is often referred to as "just in time" production.

- Supply chain representatives must select the most reliable and cost-effective suppliers. Following a financial crisis in 2012, Ford Motor Company announced plans to reduce its roster of suppliers by 40% to cut the cost of building its cars and trucks. The long-term goal was to buy parts from about 750 suppliers versus 1,260 prior to the initiative.

- Supply chain teams must be comfortable in an environment which is becoming increasingly technology-driven. Auto parts retailer O'Reilly Auto Parts owns 4,800 stores across 47 U.S. states. O'Reilly services these stores through an expansive regional distribution network that includes distribution centers and hub stores. Its inventory management and distribution systems electronically link each store to one or more distribution centers for efficient inventory control and management.

  The company operates 27 regional distribution centers which allows for same-day or overnight access to an average of 148,000 parts, many of which are not typically stocked by other retailers. The company considers this timely access to a broad range of products as a key competitive advantage to satisfying customer demand and generate repeat business.

- Supply chain pros manage complex networks of suppliers. TE Connectivity is one of the largest manufacturers of wires and connectivity components for the automotive, industrial, and electronic markets. The company manufacturers most of its products in 95 facilities located in over 20 countries. The company has stated that its products typically experience price declines of 1% to 2% per year. To offset those declines, the company constantly seeks manufacturing-process improvements at its worldwide facilities.

- Retail supply chain professionals must be attuned to consumer trends. Jeannie works in the purchasing department of a national US retailer. She is responsible for sourcing the latest shoe designs. She travels to dozens of vendors predominantly in New York City and Los Angeles to see designs and prototypes for the upcoming seasons. Jeannie then decides which shoes will be popular, taking into account different geographic preferences and price points.

- Manufacturing professionals react to fast-changing market conditions. In the second quarter of its fiscal year, semiconductor manufacturer Micron Technology reported that the average cost to produce its product increased 1%. This was bad news since there was an over-supply of product in the market, causing its average selling price to decrease 10%. Not surprisingly, the company's stock reacted poorly to the news. By the third quarter, the company developed a more efficient manufacturing process, resulting in cost reductions of 9%, almost matching an 11% decrease in its product's average sales price. By the fourth quarter, the company hit an inflection point: the average selling price decreased 6%, while the cost to produce it decreased 8%.

Practitioner #2a

OPERATIONS: FIELD OPERATIONS / CUSTOMER EXPERIENCE

Career Path	Undergraduate Degree	Advanced Degree	Personality Type	Level of Teamwork
CEO	•Operations Mgmt. •Marketing •Mgmt. Info Systems •Various other	MBA	Varies	High

Overview

This category is essentially a catchall for operational roles that support or deliver a product or service. This includes the technicians at your local cable and Internet provider, the fleet of drivers and delivery specialists at FedEx, and the pilots and customer service representatives at an airline. This would also include the operations supporting a physical retail business.

This is an extremely deep bucket that includes mostly non-business students. In fact, the top person, often known as the chief operating officer or COO, can sometimes be a non-business undergraduate major who rosc through the ranks of an operational job and went on to earn an MBA. The support team around the COO is often filled with business graduates who assist with analysis for strategy, processes, workflow, and infrastructure decisions. They also seek strategies to improve operations, position the product competitively, and enhance the end-customer experience. This extends to post-sale operations such as call centers for troubleshooting and customer service.

Field Operations: What will I do?

- Continuously analyze the customer experience
- Collaborate with marketing to learn from customer feedback and determine ways to improve service

- Manage and oversee the front lines of a company's day-to-day operations
- Focus on continuous improvement of processes and procedures to determine how operations and customer service can be faster, more efficient, and more effective
- Continuously assess field equipment, such as hand-held UPS delivery devices or a retail store's cash registers, to capture important operations and customer data
- Determine customer trends by examining data captured through transactions
- Be an expert on different channels to reach customers: digital, mobile, and physical
- Perform competitor analysis

Field Operations: What skills and qualities help?

- A "roll up your sleeves" work ethic
- Problem solver
- Ability to examine issues, consider multiple solutions, and determine most efficient choice
- Technologically savvy to work with automated or tech-enabled equipment and procedures
- Eagerness to manage larger groups

Field Operations Examples

- Field operation teams continuously focus on improving the customer experience. Consider Starbuck's transformational decision to allow customers to pre-order using the Starbucks mobile app. This allowed customers to place an order en route to a coffee shop and have their order waiting for them upon arrival, thus avoiding lengthy waits. The company also allowed customers to place orders via Amazon's Alexa voice assistant and through the Sync infotainment system on Ford vehicles.

- Field operation teams respond to increased competition. Television cable and Internet companies such as Spectrum and Comcast once enjoyed monopoly control in a market. Their reputation for customer service was often with little incentive to invest to improve the customer experience. The advent of additional service providers such as DirecTV and Verizon FiOS changed the competitive landscape and forced traditional service providers to improve their customer experience. Consumers noted the change with more specific arrival windows for field technician visits, more convenient automated scheduling functionality through a mobile app, and an increased focus on responsiveness at a company's call centers.

- Field operations professionals may manage a single office or oversee major parts of a large corporation. American Airlines' Chief Operating Officer (Robert Isom) is responsible for overseeing all aspects of the company's operations, including customer service, flight operations, maintenance, regional carrier management, cargo, safety, and security. He has undergraduate degrees in mechanical engineering and English as well as an MBA. When American Airlines merged with US Airways, Isom led the integration effort by opening a new operations center, shifting to a single reservation system, and negotiating union contracts with customer agents, fleet service, and mechanics groups.

- Field operation teams constantly assess how to improve the speed of delivery while maintaining high quality service. Canadian Pacific Railway is one of the largest railroad operators in North America with a network that extends from Vancouver to Montreal. Customers depend on the company to haul commodities such as grain, coal, and fertilizer. The company monitors over a dozen operational metrics to measure its efficiency versus the competition. One specific operational metric is known as "dwell" time—the average time a train stays at a terminal to load and unload commodities. This metric was initially an average of 8.9 hours. Management studied the terminal processes, resulting in an initial improvement to 7.5 hours the following year and 6.7 hours six years after its strategy change. The quicker turnarounds increased system capacity and generated higher company revenues.

- Field operations can touch every part of a business. Kroger is one of the country's largest food retailers with over 3,500 grocery stores, supermarkets and convenience stores. The company operates under the Kroger, Harris Teeter, Smith's, Fred Meyer, and Ralph's banners. The company has employed a "Customer 1st" business strategy for more than a decade. This strategy includes a focus on pricing, merchandising, customer service, and store layout. For store layout, the company spent billions of dollars remodeling more than 10% of its stores each year. These remodels included modernizing display cases and shelving, rearranging floor plan flows, and upgrading technology and logistics. These remodels improve the look and feel of the stores and provide an improved customer experience.

- Field operations implement new processes that can be scaled across large footprints. Home Depot's field operation's extends across more than 2,000 stores and 400,000 sales associates. The field operations' mission statement is in the form of an inverted pyramid that places customers as its top priority and executive management as the lowest priority. To improve customer service, Home Depot rolled out what it refers to as an interconnected shopping experience through a variety of initiatives that had the company:

    i. Provide associates with web-enabled handheld devices to help customers complete online sales in the aisle, expedite the checkout process, locate products, and check inventory.

    ii. Redesign its website and upgraded its mobile app to provide customers with better search capabilities and a faster checkout experience. The mobile app allows in-store customers to go online to access ratings and reviews, compare prices, view product extensions, and purchase products;

    iii. Unveil a new Customer Order Management platform ("COM") that provides a common management system for customer orders. The COM blends the online and physical shopping channels into one seamless customer experience;

iv. Introduce enhanced delivery options such as "Buy Online, Deliver From Store," "Buy Online, Pick-up In Store," and "Buy Online, Return In Store." The company also used technology to provide customers with more accurate delivery information.

The head of US operations for Home Depot, Ann-Marie Campbell, started as a cashier at a Florida store. She moved up through local and regional managerial ranks before earning her MBA and ultimately becoming executive vice president.

- Administrative operations teams are counted on to examine internal company functions and recommend cost-effective improvements. Semiconductor company Intel acquired Altera Corporation for nearly $17 billion. Altera had about 3,000 employees in the United States, United Kingdom, Malaysia, and Denmark at the time of the acquisition. After the acquisition, the companies established integration teams to focus on a smooth integration. The team included a vice president of integration planning for Altera and a vice president of strategic transactions group from Intel. The team integrated the companies to draw the best qualities from each.

Practitioner #3

STRATEGY / CORPORATE DEVELOPMENT

Career Path	Undergraduate Degree	Advanced Degree	Personality Type	Level of Teamwork
•CEO •CFO	•Finance •Strategy •Accounting •Economics	•MBA •MBA-JD	Extrovert	High

Overview

The strategy/corporate-development position collaborates with the CEO and CFO at the corporate level and the GM and product manager at the business-unit level to grow a business through mergers and acquisitions (M&A).

This person is tasked with finding potential M&A targets that can increase the scale of a business or add new product lines. M&A is also an avenue to acquire a supplier or distributor (this is known as "vertical integration"). Strategy and corporate development personnel must understand consumer trends and competitor responses to those trends. People in this role value businesses by projecting future cash flows and assigning a current value to those cash flows. The position is also responsible for finding potential buyers for assets a company may wish to sell.

A broad, in-depth understanding of a business is important because this position is expected to spot trends and capitalize on opportunities those trends present.

Strategy/Corporate Development: What will I do?

- Help determine who your company should acquire and at what price
- In conjunction with finance and operations, analyze the cost effectiveness of developing a new product or capability

versus acquiring a company that already has the product or capability

- Serve as the point person for M&A investment bankers
- Understand revenue and cost synergies – the idea that the combined efforts of two companies can add up to more than the sum of their parts. This is typically achieved by eliminating duplicate costs by consolidating overhead and personnel, commanding better terms from suppliers, and consolidating factories, office space and other real estate
- Understand valuations and concepts such as return on investment [ROI], payback period, internal rate of return [IRR], net present value [NPV] and market multiples
- Negotiate deal terms including a concept known as "earn-outs" which pays a seller a portion of a purchase price only after reaching sales milestones
- Predict future customer trends
- In conjunction with financial officials, oversee the due-diligence process—the examination of the books and records of a potential acquisition target
- Work with Treasury on the most cost effective way to finance mergers or acquisitions
- Analyze and execute the sale of unneeded company assets

Strategy/Corporate Development: What skills and qualities help?

- A "big-picture" focus
- Analytically curious
- Enjoy reviewing and evaluating businesses and business models
- Problem solver
- Enjoy negotiating and closing deals

Strategy/Corporate Development Examples

- Corporate development teams must recognize attractive acquisition candidates. Microsoft acquired LinkedIn for $26 billion.

Based on the purchase price and LinkedIn's current cash flow, it would take 13 years to recoup the investment. Microsoft's strategy and corporate development team recommended the move because it believed the company could integrate LinkedIn into Microsoft's existing customer relationship management software product (Microsoft Dynamics) for sales leads and thus increase its cash flow.

- Corporate development officials help determine the value of takeover candidates. Global yogurt and food company Danone acquired WhiteWave Foods for $12.5 billion. The purchase price represented a nearly 40x multiple of operating cash flow which is considered extremely high and indicates the expectation of dramatic growth. WhiteWave specializes in organic healthy foods and is the maker of Silk® almond milk. Danone's strategy and corporate development officials believed WhiteWave's market position combined with consumer trends toward healthy eating justified the price.

- Corporate strategists must recognize how an acquisition target can boost a business. Walt Disney acquired Pixar for $7 billion to round out its movie-studio portfolio. Disney's strategy and corporate development team recognized that in addition to movies, Disney could capitalize on Pixar characters in other parts of the company, including consumer toy products and themed rides and characters at the Disney parks.

- Strategy and corporate development teams consider many opportunities even if relatively few are executed. Honeywell's CEO, for example, stated: "At any one time we could be evaluating over 100 companies to acquire." That requires the strategy/corporate-development team to review financial statements of potential acquisition targets, determine the net present value and internal rate of return of acquiring those targets, and collaborate with business unit GMs to discuss strengths and weaknesses of the competitive landscape. Those discussions determine whether the company can build its own products or processes or if it would be wiser to acquire them.

- Strategy and corporate development teams are counted on to provide discipline to a company. Oracle decided *not* to purchase UK-based Autonomy software because the asking price was too high. Hewlett-Packard ended up paying more than $10 billion for the software but subsequently wrote off the majority of the purchase price, an admission to investors that HP overpaid for the acquisition.

- Strategy and corporate development teams identify opportunities to sell assets as well as acquire them. Pentair sold its valves-and-controls business unit to Emerson Electric for $3.15 billion because the unit no longer fit the company's strategic-growth vision. The strategy and corporate-development team likely worked for months with investment bankers to discover potential buyers and to determine an acceptable price.

- Strategy and corporate development teams are counted on to identify industry trends. Needing a better online presence and distribution infrastructure, Walmart acquired Jet.com for more than $3 billion. The company decided that spending $3 billion on Jet.com was a wiser move than focusing solely on its existing Walmart.com e-commerce platform and infrastructure.

Practitioner #4

TREASURY / RISK MANAGEMENT

Career Path	Undergraduate Degree	Advanced Degree	Personality Type	Level of Teamwork
CFO	•Finance •Accounting •Economics	•MBA •CTP •CFA •FRM	Introvert	High

Overview

The treasury department reports directly to a company's chief financial officer (CFO) and is typically comprised of three different areas:

a) <u>Cash management</u>: Treasury is central to all things cash-related within an organization, as it sets up bank accounts around the globe, tracks daily cash balances, projects future cash inflows and outflows, and invests excess cash.

b) <u>Debt management</u>: Treasury is responsible for all debt-related securities in a company's capital structure. In this capacity, treasury serves as a company's internal expert on the debt and interest-rate markets. As the internal company expert on the debt markets, the treasurer is responsible for raising money through bank loans or from the bond markets when a company needs to raise non-equity capital.

c) <u>Risk management</u>: The risk management area is vast. Sometimes it is a direct piece of the treasury team. In these instances, risk management is responsible for insurance and financial derivative planning for commodities and currencies. Risk management also extends to enterprise planning for counter-party risk and a term known as "VaR" (value-at-risk). In some situations, risk management can fall outside of the direct purview of a treasury team and be more suited for a quantitative background.

In total, these three areas are typically known as asset-liability management, or ALM.

The treasury team serves at the corporate level and also works with the financial planning and analysis (FP&A) teams to project future revenue and costs. It also works with back-office operations to determine cash uses, sources, and needs.

Treasury: What will I do?

- Oversee cash management—open global bank accounts and oversee investments of cash
- Work with business-unit general managers and FP&A teams to determine funding requirements for budgets
- Serve as the internal expert on the debt, currency, commodity, and interest-rate markets, to determine when market conditions are most favorable
- Serve as the point person to raise debt in the bond and bank markets. Will be responsible for preparing offering memorandums and slide decks detailing a deal's terms and investment considerations
- Hedge interest-rate, foreign currency, and commodity exposures and be an expert on derivative instruments, such as fixed-floating swaps, cross-currency swaps, forward contracts, and collars
- Work closely with the company's strategy and corporate development team and investment bankers to consider the best ways to finance possible mergers or acquisitions
- Help oversee a company's insurance coverage and work closely with the real estate team on office leases, surety bonds, and letters of credit
- Serve as the main point of contact for rating agencies and commercial bankers

Treasury: What skills and qualities help?

- Attention to detail
- Enjoy working with money
- Enjoy working with numbers
- Tolerate repetitive monthly work
- Enjoy a role that can require less travel than many other business roles
- Adept at saving money
- Enjoy having a bird's-eye view of a company rather than deep involvement in business-unit operations

Treasury Examples

- Treasury professionals need a thorough understanding of the most advantageous financial actions for a company. When Microsoft acquired LinkedIn for $26 billion it raised $20 billion in corporate bonds with maturities ranging from three to 40 years. At first glance, it seemed odd that Microsoft would borrow the money when it had more than $110 billion in cash and short-term investments. The treasury team recognized that much of that money was held overseas. Bringing it back to the United States would incur hefty tax payments. The team recognized that borrowing the money was the more prudent move.
- Treasury team members need to be aware of the details of a company's financial moves. In 2016, Fidelity National Information Services borrowed $3 billion from a group of banks. The interest rate on the loan was based on the company's credit ratings. The agreement also tied the level of the company's debt to its cash flow. Treasury officials made sure the company qualified for the best interest rate and stayed within the agreed debt agreements.
- Treasury professionals at international companies must be aware of the impacts of foreign currency markets. Corning Incorporated is one of the world's leading manufacturers of glass screens for the television industry. The majority of its clients (TV makers

such as Samsung, Sony, and LG) are located in Asia so Corning has a large currency exposure to the Japanese yen and Korean won. To adjust for that, the treasury team buys foreign currency derivatives to limit Corning's financial volatility from fluctuating currency rates. This strategy gives management greater certainty around pricing and costs.

- Treasury is important for cities, states, and other public entities as well as corporations. The city of Louisville and Jefferson County in Kentucky issued $175 million in tax-exempt bonds priced at a yield of 3.4%. The bonds are "revenue bonds" and are secured by future payments by residents for water, sewer, and drainage services.

- Treasury teams can save companies significant sums by understanding capital markets. In 2016, SiriusXM paid off many of its bonds four years early. The decision was made due to historically low interest rates. The treasury team determined that the lower interest rates on new loans would more than offset the pre-payment penalty the company paid for calling in its existing bonds early.

- Treasury officials must protect the companies they serve through prudent financial management. Agriculture company Monsanto had over $1.7 billion in cash and short-term securities on its balance sheet. The company invested the cash in deposits with major banks or money-market funds throughout the world in high-quality, short-term debt instruments. The company invested limited amounts in each institution to minimize counter-party risk.

- Risk management helps limit volatility from external sources. Archer-Daniels-Midland (ADM) is one of the world's leading processors of corn, wheat, and other commodities. Crop prices fluctuate widely due to changes in weather conditions, crop diseases, government subsidies, and overall global supply-demand trends. In order to limit volatility, ADM has global teams monitor commodity positions and prices against management-established limits.

Practitioner #5

FINANCIAL PLANNING & ANALYSIS

Career Path	Undergraduate Degree	Advanced Degree	Personality Type	Level of Teamwork
CFO	•Accounting •Finance •Economics •Mgt. Info Systems	•MBA •CMA •CPA •MS in Finance	Extrovert	High

Overview

Financial planning and analysis, typically referred to as FP&A, is another direct lieutenant to the chief financial officer (CFO). The FP&A department pulls together information throughout a corporation to help with budgets and projections. It supplies information to decision makers on how changes in pricing, employment, overhead, research and development, and other items will impact a company's financial performance.

Roles within FP&A can vary from a very junior level, where an individual is responsible for tracking a few line items, such as the amount a company spends on corporate travel, to a more senior role serving as a direct partner with the business unit general manager (GM) to steer the business through major decisions.

FP&A personnel assist the CFO, product managers, business development leaders, and other decision makers across the organization with the financial analysis and data to make wise investment decisions.

Financial Planning & Analysis: What will I do?

- Serve as the point person for budgets, projections, and tracking key performance measures

- Aggregate business unit budgets into one top-level corporate budget
- Work with general managers to explain variances. A company's accounting group may report that revenue increased from $100 million to $150 million. It's up to FP&A to help explain why it increased by $50 million
- Track key performance indicators (KPIs) that help determine a business's health such as changes in pricing, volume, regional performance, or specific brand performance
- Prioritize capital projects to determine how a company should invest its resources. When deciding between different projects, FP&A will calculate the internal rate of return (IRR) and net present value (NPV) of cash flows to determine how long it will take to earn those investments back and compare the rates of return for each choice.
- Serve as a business-unit CFO to advise that unit's GM and product manager
- Perform economic and financial analysis for routine company business decisions
- Perform "build-versus-buy" analysis to determine whether it makes more sense for a company to build a product or to acquire it from a supplier or through an acquisition.
- Collaborate with strategy, sales, human resources and others to calculate an acquisition's total impact. This includes projecting cost savings and potential for increased sales.
- Work closely with accounting, tax, and treasury on corporate-level budgets and projections
- Perform competitor analysis
- Understand financial and accounting software and systems, such as SAP and Oracle

Financial Planning & Analysis: What skills and qualities help?

- Attention to detail
- Enjoy working with numbers

- Enjoy building large, detailed financial models that project multiple years and include advanced functions such as pivot and lookup tables
- Tolerate repetitive monthly work
- Good team person who can be counted on for support

Financial Planning and Analysis Examples

- FP&A teams help companies make informed strategic decisions. Prior to launching its popular Prime membership and annual Prime Day event, Amazon's FP&A team ran profit-and-loss projections to show the impact on the company's financial statements to internal decision makers. The team's projections likely illustrated a variety of scenarios using different pricing and volume scenarios.
- FP&A personnel provide key projections to help companies make investment decisions. Traditional phone company Verizon Communications decided to roll out its television service (FiOS) in 2005. The company ultimately spent upward of $20 billion building the cable infrastructure across the country. Verizon's FP&A team was likely critical in helping operational decision makers determine the timeline, how much to invest, which markets to prioritize, and the overall impact to corporate financial results.
- FP&A teams provide important financial information to investors on a regular basis. Each quarter, the FP&A team at industrial-equipment manufacturer Caterpillar provides details about changes in revenue and expenses. Revenue changes are broken down by volume, price, and currency. Changes in expenses are detailed by variable costs such as volume, price, and currency, as well as fixed costs such as manufacturing and overhead expenses. This material gives a clear picture of the company's performance.
- FP&A teams help internal decision makers understand geographic trends and plan production. Each month, the head of

FP&A for the Asia region of global soft-drink maker ABC Cola reports 12-month historical sales. She also projects the 12 months ahead. The report is used to plan production by the global head of FP&A, the treasurer, and the chief financial officer who combine it with projections from Europe, South America, Africa, and North America to estimate future company cash inflows and outflows.

- FP&A helps companies set priorities. Big Box Retailer ABC-Mart wants to upgrade multiple areas of its business, including its inventory software, its credit-card-terminal systems, its online website, and its in-store display cases. The company's FP&A team has projected that all the projects will cost $2 billion. But the company can spend only $1 billion. The FP&A team will present financial projections and the net present value of each project to the CFO and CEO to determine which will have the highest return on investment (ROI) potential.

- FP&A professionals often work with strict deadlines. Shawn is a junior member of an FP&A team for a public pharmaceutical company. During the last week of each fiscal quarter, he spends late nights working with his colleagues in accounting to reconcile journal entries and bank statements. He also spends late nights working on slide presentations during the week leading up to the company's quarterly earnings conference call.

Practitioner #5a

CORPORATE ACCOUNTING

Career Path	Undergraduate Degree	Advanced Degree	Personality Type	Level of Teamwork
CFO	Accounting	•CPA •MS in Accounting	Introvert	High

Overview

Unlike all other careers discussed in this book, people pursuing a corporate accounting career *must* have an accounting degree. Plenty of people working in finance, for example, did not receive a finance degree. But given the highly technical nature of the work, the same cannot be said for accounting.

An accounting degree has become a five-year endeavor at many colleges and the CPA designation has become more crucial in the corporate accounting and audit careers than probably any other advanced degree or certification discussed in this book. The rules for obtaining the CPA are also unusually rigid with very specific college credits and work experience requirements. **Despite these hurdles, an accounting background and CPA designation open up a world of opportunities, especially for people interested in becoming a chief financial officer (CFO).**

The accounting role is highly integrated into all company business procedures so the field shouldn't be considered through a narrow prism. An accounting career's main focus revolves around preparing financial statements using generally accepted accounting principles (GAAP). The accounting team is responsible for recording every transaction, such as a sale to a customer or a payment to a vendor, and making the appropriate journal entries into the general ledger, usually an elaborate software system that records all sale and cost transactions. This information is used to produce monthly financial statements that summarize a company's transactions. The statements are of great interest to company officials and to lenders and investors. The accounting team is ultimately responsible for ensuring the statements accurately reflect a company's financial position.

"Controller" or "Chief Accounting Officer" is the title typically given to the top accounting officer. This individual is a key lieutenant to the CFO. Many CFOs will have experience as a controller and many business unit CFOs will either be staffed by a junior controller or a financial planning and analysis (FP&A) professional.

In addition to preparing financial statements, the accounting team has a corporate-tax function. The tax group makes sure the company pays the appropriate taxes. The group also helps determine strategies to minimize taxes. The tax implications of many company decisions can materially affect the return on investment. Consequently, tax issues play a major role in significant company decisions. This tax role is highly specialized and therefore falls outside of the scope of this book.

Corporate Accounting: What will I do?

- Record journal entries (debits and credits) into a general ledger
- Stay current on all accounting rules as determined by the group that sets the standards, the Financial Accounting Standards Board (FASB)
- Prepare financial statements
- Work with the FP&A and treasury groups to explain footnotes and analysis included in financial statements
- Work as key contact person for auditors
- Perform purchase accounting: allocating the purchase price of an acquisition towards assets on the balance sheet such as property, plant & equipment (PP&E), Intangible assets, and goodwill
- Understand financial and accounting software and systems such as SAP and Oracle
- Maintain CPA standing by earning annual continuing education credits

Corporate Accounting: What skills and qualities help?

- Enjoy solving the puzzle-like aspect of debits and credits
- Detail oriented
- Tolerate work that can be repetitive or tedious at times, especially early in the career
- Tolerate long hours at times such as the end of each quarter
- Enjoy working with numbers
- Prefer not to travel a great deal

Corporate Accounting Examples:

- Accountants often work with strict deadlines. Wendy is an accountant for a public pharmaceutical company. During the last week of each fiscal quarter, she spends late nights making final debits and credits and reviews important financial statement footnotes with the FP&A and treasury teams. She does this in order to close the books on time to file statements with the Securities & Exchange Commission (SEC).
- Accountants play a crucial role in creating a clear picture for investors. Walt Disney's accounting department prepares the company's unaudited quarterly financial statements known as Form 10-Q and the annual audited statements known as Form 10-K. They include an income statement, balance sheet and cash-flow statement, footnotes, and the Management's Discussion and Analysis. These statements are closely followed by investors and lenders to determine the value and creditworthiness of Disney.
- The accounting team must have a good understanding about the proper recording of revenues, expenses, assets, and liabilities. Global software company Oracle Corporation has a wide array of products including databases, software applications, services, and hardware. All software products can be delivered at a company's location or through the cloud. The company recognizes revenue for each product or service as stated by Generally Accepting Accounting Principles (GAAP), the rules of accounting. The

company's financial reports include pages of detail written by the accounting department describing their procedures for recording various sales. Many have important nuances that are closely watched by investors and lenders.

- The accounting team often collaborates in preparing financial projections. In 2016, industrial company Pentair sold its valves-and-controls business unit to Emerson Electric. As a result of the sale, the FP&A group and the accounting teams revised full-year forecasts to reflect lost cash flows from the business which were partially offset by lower interest expense. The company told investors to expect lower earnings per share (EPS) in the following year than they had projected before the divestiture.

- Accounting teams are highly necessary for the investment world. Asset managers need accountants to properly record gains and losses from security sales, as well as to properly record interest income and dividend income on security holdings. This extends further to accounting for the tax impact of those situations as well.

Practitioner #6

INVESTOR RELATIONS

Career Path	Undergraduate Degree	Advanced Degree	Personality Type	Level of Teamwork
CFO	•Finance •Accounting •Strategy •Economics	•MBA •CFA	Extrovert	High

Overview

Investor relations (IR) serves as the company liaison to existing and prospective investors. The investor relations team sets up meetings, attends and speaks at industry conferences, and communicates with investors and external analysts when they have questions about a company's operations or financial status. Investor relations personnel keep abreast of all things about a company including its product development, marketing, sales, financial performance, competitor performance, stock performance, and valuations. The head of investor relations serves as a direct lieutenant to a company's CEO and CFO.

Investor Relations: What will I do?

- Maintain a bird's-eye view of a company, understanding all aspects of the business in detail
- Serve as the main contact for shareholders, investors, and equity analysts. Function as a "generalist": knowledgeable on many subjects with the ability to bring in product managers and other experts when greater detail is required by an investor.
- Maintain knowledge of shareholder base: know who is buying or selling shares, why they are buying or selling, and what their history is with other companies
- Coordinate quarterly and annual earnings calls and other shareholder events

- Coordinate and participate in speaking engagements at industry and analyst conferences
- Stay abreast of a company's performance and valuations in relation to industry competitors
- Work with Communications and PR departments on issuing press releases and company announcements

Investor Relations: What skills and qualities help?

- Enjoy frequent interaction with parties such as investors and analysts
- Ability to understand and explain complicated business strategies
- Enjoy public speaking

Investor Relations Examples

- Investor relations officials help explain a company's business to investors and other interested parties. Tyler works in investor relations for a publicly-traded global pharmaceutical company. As part of his responsibilities, he organizes internal quarterly meetings with general managers and chief financial officers of the company's four business units to stay current on the latest business strategies and financial results. He uses these meetings as informational sessions to prepare for the flurry of inquiries he typically receives from shareholders and analysts.
- Tyler also leads or co-leads with the chief executive officer dozens of meetings every year with investors. At these meetings, Tyler answers questions on every aspect of his company, including business strategy, financial results, future guidance, and other nuances that interest investors.
- Investor relations personnel need to have a comprehensive understanding of a company's operations. James and Nancy work in investor relations for ABC Corporation, a public company

that manufactures and distributes paper products such as cups, plates, and tissues. Lori and Steven work in financial planning and analysis at the same company. They function as the business-unit chief financial officer (CFO) overseeing the finances of the domestic and international divisions. Each quarter, the four meet with ABC's chief executive officer and corporate CFO to prepare for their quarterly earnings calls. The meetings last about three hours and include dozens of Excel spread sheets highlighting year-over-year and quarter-over-quarter changes on each source of revenue and expenses. The sheets also include items such as the volume of shipments, average pricing, average headcount, and average compensation. The goal is to prepare for questions investment analysts may ask so they can provide accurate and informative responses.

- Investor relations are responsible for organizing important company events. ABC Corporation also holds an "Analyst Day" each year. The event provides a detailed look inside the company's businesses and includes formal presentations by the chief executive officer, chief financial officer, and general managers of the company's two main business units. The investor relations department must prepare the event and ensure that all interested parties are invited.

Practitioner #7

HUMAN RESOURCES / HUMAN CAPITAL

Career Path	Undergraduate Degree	Advanced Degree	Personality Type	Level of Teamwork
MD/Partner	Various	MBA	Extrovert	High

Overview

The human resources role is responsible for recruiting, screening, and developing a company's workforce and functions as a partner to the business units and departments within an organization.

To succeed in this role, you must thoroughly understand the needs of the business unit and overall company strategy. You also need a firm grasp on the qualifications required to fill vacant positions. Responsibilities include developing a pool of candidates for key roles. This is often achieved by working with recruiting firms.

In addition to finding and hiring employees, human resources is responsible for employee-benefit plans, employee training, and employee educational programs. It also takes a lead role when employment needs to be reduced or when conflicts are addressed.

Human Resources: What will I do?

- Assist business managers with drafting employment requisitions (known as "job recs") including job descriptions and desired qualifications to use in recruitment and screening
- Screen employment candidates to select candidates for interviews
- Develop expertise in compensation and benefit issues and stay current on industry compensation trends

- Develop relationship with recruiting and staffing firms and build awareness of online recruiting resources
- Develop a pipeline with key employment resources such as college career centers
- Oversee employee training programs
- Resolve work-related conflicts
- Develop policies and procedures around time away, child care, social media, community service, and many other work-life balance issues

Human Resources: What skills and qualities help?

- Strong organizational skills
- Enjoy meeting with people
- Ability to understand people, assess talent, and match job seekers with available positions
- Ability to deal with multiple constituents while working under tight deadlines
- Diplomatic skills required to deliver unwelcome news in a professional manner such as employment termination
- Good crisis-management skills

Human Resources Examples

- Human resources must collaborate with other departments to understand their staffing needs. Mickey works in human resources for a global consumer-products company. The company has 20,000 employees located throughout the world. Mickey is specifically responsible for the North America finance and accounting groups. He collaborates with managers across the treasury, financial planning and analysis, and accounting departments to gather information on desired qualities for new candidates.
- Human resources personnel need to develop an expertise in company benefits. Blake works in human resources for a major

investment bank. He is responsible for benefits such as health insurance, the 401(k) retirement plan, and vacation policy. He hosts information sessions for new employees to explain those programs and is the resource for addressing those topics when questions arise.

- Human resources personnel are counted on to spearhead all college and professional recruiting strategies. This includes establishing relationships with key universities to develop internship pipelines and to recruit for entry-level positions. Human resources also collaborates with recruiting firms to provide insight on a firm's open positions.

Practitioner #8

AUDITOR

Career Path	Undergraduate Degree	Advanced Degree	Personality Type	Level of Teamwork
•MD/Partner •CFO	Accounting	•CPA •MS in Accounting •MS in Tax •LLM in Tax	Introvert	High

Note: these boxes are for the External Audit career

Overview

An auditor aims to confirm that a company's financial statements accurately reflect its financial condition. It's a role that is extremely important to a company's investors and lenders since it is expected to be an unbiased, third-party assessment. There are two types of auditors:

a) <u>External Auditor</u>: these are the auditors employed by the "Big 4"—Ernst & Young, KPMG, PWC, and Deloitte & Touch—as well as smaller firms such as Grant Thornton and BDO. A career in external audit almost always requires having a degree in accounting which has become a five-year endeavor at many colleges. Additionally, a Certified Public Accounting (CPA) designation is more essential in the audit and corporate accounting fields than probably any other advanced degree or certification discussed in this book.

 The external audit team confirms the work of the accounting and treasury teams. They check that a company's accounting procedures follow Generally Accepted Accounting Principles (GAAP) and confirm that financial inflows and outflows to employees, vendors, suppliers, and customers are properly tracked and recorded. The ultimate purpose of an external audit team is to "sign off" on a company's financial statements to validate that the statements, risk factors, and processes are accurately documented and represented.

A career in external auditing follows a specific path. Less experienced auditors perform the more tedious work of an account while more seasoned team members tackle more material areas of a business and supervise junior staff. Some auditors stay in the profession and seek to earn partner status. Others use it as a stepping stone to other financial work and pursue the chief financial officer career path. This is achieved by leaving the audit field and moving in to one of the roles discussed earlier—corporate accounting, financial planning and analysis, or strategy/corporate development. The skills learned in an external audit career, such as financial statement analysis, can be helpful in buy-side, hedge fund, private equity and sell-side analyst careers.

b) Internal Auditor: these are the auditors employed in-house by the CFO. Among other things, their responsibility is to assure that all internal "controls" are in place and properly functioning. These controls include making sure the internal information systems work properly and are not easily susceptible to errors or fraud. This role is heavily tied to Congress's Sarbanes-Oxley Act of 2002, which requires executive management to attest to the accuracy of their financial statements. The ultimate career path within internal audit is limited but the role can lead towards one of the other financial or operational careers discussed earlier since it touches many areas of a business.

Auditor: What will I do?

- Review the work of the accounting, treasury, and other financial departments to confirm procedures comply with GAAP
- Review bank-account statements to verify inflows and outflow of funds
- Have a strong understanding of your client's business model and industry

- Confirm payments and receipts between vendors, suppliers, employees, and customers
- Check internal processes to avoid fraud and mistakes
- Keep informed of all new accounting regulations and standards

Auditor: What skills and qualities help?

- Attention to detail
- Adept at understanding financial systems that record and facilitate financial transactions
- Adept at "following the money" such as the inflows and outflows of cash and tracking those transactions back to financial statements
- Enjoy working with numbers
- Tolerate sometimes tedious work
- Willing to travel

Auditor Examples

- Paying close attention to detail is an important part of an auditors' work. Nicole is a junior auditor for a boutique audit firm located on the East Coast. She is responsible for auditing a portfolio of media and entertainment clients. Her assignment includes a two-week trip to the Hollywood headquarters of her client to audit their cash management and treasury functions. This includes analyzing monthly bank statements, verifying all major cash deposits and cash withdrawals, and confirming that vendors are legitimate. She also verifies that appropriate debits and credits are made for each transaction and confirms bank accounts contain accurate amounts.
- External auditors must express an opinion about the condition of a company's financial statement. The opinions are carefully-worded and are closely followed by investors and lenders. Below is Deloitte & Touche's audit opinion included in Microsoft's annual 10-K SEC filing in 2017:

REPORT OF INDEPENDENT REGISTERED PUBLIC ACCOUNTING FIRM

To the Board of Directors and Stockholders of Microsoft Corporation
Redmond, Washington

We have audited the accompanying consolidated balance sheets of Microsoft Corporation and subsidiaries (the "Company") as of June 30, 2017 and 2016, and the related consolidated statements of income, comprehensive income, cash flows, and stockholders' equity for each of the three years in the period ended June 30, 2017. These financial statements are the responsibility of the Company's management. Our responsibility is to express an opinion on these financial statements based on our audits.

We conducted our audits in accordance with the standards of the Public Company Accounting Oversight Board (United States). Those standards require that we plan and perform the audit to obtain reasonable assurance about whether the financial statements are free of material misstatement. An audit includes examining, on a test basis, evidence supporting the amounts and disclosures in the financial statements. An audit also includes assessing the accounting principles used and significant estimates made by management, as well as evaluating the overall financial statement presentation. We believe that our audits provide a reasonable basis for our opinion.

In our opinion, such consolidated financial statements present fairly, in all material respects, the financial position of Microsoft Corporation and subsidiaries as of June 30, 2017 and 2016, and the results of their operations and their cash flows for each of the three years in the period ended June 30, 2017, in conformity with accounting principles generally accepted in the United States of America.

We have also audited, in accordance with the standards of the Public Company Accounting Oversight Board (United States), the Company's internal control over financial reporting as of June 30, 2017, based on the criteria established in *Internal Control – Integrated Framework (2013)* issued by the Committee of Sponsoring Organizations of the Treadway Commission and our report dated August 2, 2017 expressed an unqualified opinion on the Company's internal control over financial reporting.

/s/   DELOITTE & TOUCHE LLP
Seattle, Washington
August 2, 2017

- Auditors must identify deficiencies they find in company financial processes. When Warner Music became a stand-alone public entity after being privately owned for many years its auditors performed internal-control tests to make sure the company's operations had the proper checks and balances to detect mistakes or fraud. As a result of its auditor's review, Warner included the following statement in its 10-K SEC filing:

Changes in Internal Control over Financial Reporting

In connection with our last fiscal year audit, our auditors noted a material weakness related to our U.S. Recorded Music royalty payable balance, noting that our domestic operations used different royalty systems which created certain complexities in reconciling royalties payable. During this fiscal year, we remediated the material weakness. In connection with this remediation, we implemented additional monitoring controls and improved the quality of supporting documentation to substantiate certain accruals and royalty balances. There have been no other changes in our Internal Controls over financial reporting or other factors during this fiscal year that have materially affected, or are reasonably likely to materially affect, our Internal Controls.

Bucket #2: Analysts

W hile the practitioners bucket generally features structured management, large teams, and matrix reporting, the analysts bucket is characterized mostly by individual work and small teams.

The careers in this bucket usually are employed by financial and investment organizations. These are different from the "product" companies we focused on in the practitioner section. Understanding the financial and investment organizations that employ most of these careers is important. These companies are typically divided into three areas: a front office, middle office, and back office. As you might imagine, the front-office jobs are the highest profile and most lucrative and are the focus of this section.

- Front Office: Analysts (the focus of this section), traders (discussed in "Bucket #3: Matchmakers"), and portfolio managers
- Middle Office: Financial planning and analysis (FP&A) and risk management (both covered in "Bucket #1: Practitioner") and legal/compliance, which are beyond the scope of this book. The risk management area for financial and investment companies is responsible for value-at-risk ("VaR") which entails monitoring the exposure to counter-party risk. A company, for example, may set strict limits on the amount an analyst can buy in any one stock or do business with any one company.
- Back Office: Data management, cash management, operations, accounting, and tax (all covered at least briefly in "Bucket #1: Practitioner")

What Is Asset Management?

Asset management is a term widely used in financial circles and is associated with all of the careers discussed in this section. Simply put, money is the asset being managed. People, companies, and numerous other organizations with money could simply place it in a savings account at their local bank or even keep it under their mattress if they chose. But recognizing that there is greater opportunity available, most people and organizations seek other options. This is where asset management comes in.

When it comes to careers, think of asset managers as the employers and the titles discussed in this section as the actual careers. A mutual fund, for example, is considered an asset manager and employs buy-side analysts and economists. Hedge funds, insurance companies, pension funds, university endowments, and sovereign wealth funds all fit this role as well. Additionally, private equity and venture capital firms are also considered asset managers.

The "Bucket #2: Analyst" section looks at the careers in isolation but you should realize that there can be some overlap among them. Buy-side investors, private equity, hedge funds, and venture capitalists can invest in similar areas. Additionally, you should be aware that even product companies such as Google and Intel have their own venture-capital and investment arms.

Finally, the careers in this section can have many different titles and names. For example, a buy-side analyst can often be called a research analyst. Because of this abundance of titles, I list a set of "also known as" for each career. The differences are in title only. The overall substance, job descriptions, and personality traits are identical.

A Little Background on Equity, Debt, and Other Capital Markets

Before diving into specific analyst careers, it is important to understand a few concepts about how companies are financed along with the capital markets in which they operate.

First, recognize that a business needs capital to get started. Capital is usually money that pays for office or factory space, equipment, supplies, and employee salaries before a company is generating sufficient funds. Capital is also needed when companies expand or build new plants. Capital can take two forms: equity or debt.

Equity:

The most common form of capital raised by a company is equity. It can be private, such as the initial funds family and friends give someone who is starting a business or the money a venture capitalist provides to support a start-up idea. It can also be public if it is raised as an initial public offering (IPO) and subsequently traded in the public markets.

In return for providing funds, investors receive "equity" or ownership in a company. This might entitle them to vote on important decisions or receive periodic payments known as dividends if the company earns enough money to pay them. Additionally, as owners, holders of common equity, enjoy the appreciation when a company becomes more valuable. Early investors in Amazon, for example, have seen their investments grow exponentially. On the downside, if a company goes bankrupt, equity holders are usually last in line to receive any liquidation proceeds and can see their entire investment disappear.

There are various nuances within the equity category, such as preferred equity and super-voting shares. For the purposes of this book, we will focus on regular common equity, also known as common stock.

One more point on equity is that while the majority of focus is on owning the equity and hoping a company does well (known as "long" equity), it is also possible to bet against a company. Investors "short" equity when they believe a company's stock is overpriced and that it will eventually fall. In this case, investors borrow stock from a long investor, sell it, and buy it back at a later date at what they hope to be a lower price. If the prediction of a stock price decline is correct, the "short" investor walks away with a profit.

Consequently, it can be valuable for analysts to predict not only which companies will fare well but also to be able to identify companies that may struggle.

Debt:

The other way a company can raise capital is by borrowing money from a bank or through the bond markets. The reasons companies issue debt are vast and can range from acquiring another company, building a new plant, investing in a new product, expanding into new regions, or even paying dividends, or making share repurchases.

The principal difference between issuing equity and debt is that an equity holder has an ownership stake in a company while a debt holder is a lender and will receive an agreed-upon rate of interest for lending money to a company. Debt holders have the advantage of being ahead of equity holders in line for remaining assets when a company goes bankrupt.

The concept of "collateral" is a crucial part of the debt markets. This refers to lenders being able to have claims on a company's assets with the company legally restricted from giving that collateral to anyone else. Think of a home mortgage from a bank—a homeowner would never be allowed to pledge their home to someone ahead of the bank's claim. The same concept applies to the corporate bond world.

While the equity markets are pretty straightforward despite having categories such as common, preferred, and super-voting shares, the debt markets become more nuanced with various layers and structures.

It is important to be aware of the synonyms used when talking about debt markets. Fixed income is another word for debt instruments because it typically pays a *fixed* recurring amount, known as interest coupon. The terms "bond," "fixed income," "credit," "loans," and "debt" are essentially all interchangeable terms and are used that way in this book and in the real world.

These terms simply refer to someone lending money to someone else, such as a corporation, a city, or a real-estate owner, with the expectation they will be paid interest at a recurring period, usually twice a year. The principal part of the loan is typically paid back either through periodic payments or, more commonly, with a single balloon payment at the end of the loan period.

To help make the examples discussed in the coming pages more understandable, use this brief description of the different types of debt instruments:

- **Investment-Grade (IG) Bonds:** Investment-grade bonds are debt raised by larger, more financially solid companies. The term "investment grade" signifies a high credit quality (think similar to a consumer with an admirable FICO score). IG bonds are typically unsecured which means they are not supported by a particular asset.
- **High-Yield (HY) Bonds:** Sometimes referred to as Junk Bonds, high-yield bonds are debt raised by smaller or lower-credit-quality companies. The lower credit quality means the investor receives higher interest rates compared to investment-grade bonds. Unlike investment-grade bonds, high-yield bonds are often secured by assets.
- **Bank Term Loans:** Also known as leveraged loans, these are a bank's equivalent of a high-yield bond. It is a bank loan to a lower-credit-quality company that is almost always secured or guaranteed with strict terms and conditions.
- **Bridge Loans:** These are temporary loans granted by a group of banks. These are often used for mergers and acquisitions. The goal is for these loans to be used for a specific transaction that has an approaching deadline. Bridge loans provide a company one less thing to worry about when closing a large transaction since it provides a commitment for financing. The goal is for the borrower to issue longer term bonds once the specific transaction closes to pay back the bridge loan.
- **Bank Revolvers:** Similar to a credit line on a credit card, bank revolvers are revolving credit facilities that corporations use when they need money. The corporation pays interest only on the amount borrowed. The interest rate floats, so it rises and falls with general market rates. The term revolver comes from the

ability to borrow and pay back the loan without impacting the total amount available.

- **Asset-Based Loans:** Asset-based loans are similar to leveraged loans except that these loans are legally tied to specific pools of assets such as accounts receivable, inventory, or equipment. These loans typically only have claims on those particular assets. To limit risk, lenders will typically make loans for a fraction of the assets available. A bank may offer only a $50 million loan on $100 million of inventory, for example. By doing that, the bank increases its likelihood of being paid back even if a company struggles to sell all inventory or if the underlying collateral depreciates in value.
- **Middle Market Loans:** A generic term for loans made to smaller companies. Some asset managers, for example, specialize in loans to companies with revenue of $100 million or less. This compares to some of the nation's largest companies that generate tens of billions of dollars in revenues.
- **Convertible Corporate Bonds:** Convertible corporate bonds are similar to regular corporate bonds with an important difference: the bonds typically pay a lower rate of interest since the bond holder will have the opportunity to convert the debt into equity if a borrower's stock price exceeds a predetermined target. This provides some of the safety of debt with some of the upside potential of equity.
- **Structured Debt:** Structured debt is legally secured by pools of recurring cash flows. These pools come in many forms: mortgage payments, student-loan payments, auto-loan payments, and credit-card payments to name a few. The originator of these loans will package them into a diverse pool, divide them by payment priority, and resell them to investors. For example, Citibank may take $1 billion of different mortgages from different states and package them to sell to an investor, who then earns interest and principal payments. The most common types of structured debt are commercial and residential mortgage-backed securities (CMBS and RMBS), asset-backed securities (ABS), and collateralized

loan obligations (CLO), where banks will package their loan portfolios and sell them off to investors.

- **Public Debt:** Public debt is similar to corporate debt except that instead of involving a corporation such as Facebook or Apple, the borrower is a government, municipality, country, or an affiliated entity such as a government agency, hospital, or airport. The transactions are usually secured by future tax, utility, or other types of payments by local residents. This category may include large infrastructure projects such as new bridges that will be repaid by auto tolls, new schools that will be repaid by property taxes and water and sewer projects that will be paid by future fees or taxes

- **Distressed Debt:** Distressed debt is the term given to the bonds and loans of a company that is in or near bankruptcy. This debt was initially issued with the expectation that it will be paid back in full. But as business conditions change, such as a newspaper company losing subscribers due to the Internet, the prospects of being paid back the full amount disappears. Investors in this area seek what is known as recovery value. They look for loans where the assets of the company are worth more than what the market is valuing them. Since companies with distressed debt are typically near bankruptcy, an investor can purchase the debt at a significant discount. If an investor judges correctly they can receive substantially more than what they paid. If the situation is worse than they project, the debt may be worth less than the purchase amount and in some cases it may be worth nothing.

Derivatives (Forwards, Futures, Options, Swaps, Collars):

Derivatives are contracts between buyers and sellers, usually for something in the future. Call options on stocks are a common type of derivative. They allow a buyer to purchase a stock at a set price at some point in the future with a limit on the downside. Someone who believes the stock will drop would be eager to sell a call option while someone who expects the stock to rise would be a buyer of that type of derivative. A contract to change a floating interest rate to a fixed rate is another type of derivative as is a contract to lock in future rates for foreign currencies or commodity prices. Derivatives are usually used by sophisticated investors or companies to hedge their risk.

Emerging Markets:
Emerging markets refers to the capital markets for less-developed countries that are exhibiting strong growth and have the potential to become more advanced. Countries such as Brazil, Russia, India, and China (sometimes referred to as "BRIC's") are notable emerging markets. Companies within emerging markets need investors and access to stable capital markets such as those found in the U.S. For example, Chinese e-commerce giant Alibaba has issued equity and debt in the U.S. markets. Bilingual individuals can make a particular impact in specializing in emerging markets.

> *This brief overview of the types of debt and instruments used in the financial world will help you understand the careers in the following pages. You will notice some overlap for people working in different capital markets. The work will have similarities but you will find separate analysts, traders, economists and bankers for equities, corporate bonds, public bonds, currencies, commodities, and emerging markets just to name a few!*

Know the Language: Buy-side versus Sell-side

Buckets #2 and #3 spend a lot of time discussing buy-side and sell-side careers. These are common terms used throughout the asset management and banking industries. The "buy-side" is fairly simple to understand. It refers to people that have money to invest and therefore *buy* assets and securities. This is typically one of the asset managers we discuss in this section. For example, an asset manager may buy 100 shares of Microsoft stock.

THE ULTIMATE CAREER GUIDE FOR BUSINESS MAJORS

The "sell-side" refers to the roles that *sell or broker* transactions, as well as roles that write research used by the buy-side. Using the same 100 Microsoft shares, the sell-side will include the traders that executed the sale and the institutional sales individuals that service the asset manager who bought the shares. Going a step further, let's assume an asset manager bought the shares because he read a favorable report on Microsoft from a *sell-side* analyst and a favorable economic report from a *sell-side* economist. Finally, let's assume the 100 shares were issued in a new stock offering from Microsoft. In that case, the investment bankers that advised Microsoft on the stock offering can also be considered sell-side.

As you can see from this example, the sell-side is focused on anything that can facilitate a transaction. These characteristics of buy-side and sell-side should crystallize as you read the pages ahead.

Portfolio Managers (PM) = Mini-CIO

Similar to the general managers who function as mini-chief executive officers in the practitioners bucket, the analysts bucket has a similar concept known as portfolio managers (PMs). Each asset management firm may have multiple portfolio managers responsible for different sub-segments of investing who all report up to the chief investment officer (CIO). One portfolio manager may oversee equities while another oversees US bonds and another for emerging market bonds.

The portfolio manager oversees how a portfolio is constructed and will determine the appropriate weightings of different industries and types of investments. This person is usually the ultimate decision maker for buy-and-sell transactions. Their main goal is to outperform the broader market. An investment that delivers stronger returns than a widely followed index, such as the S&P 500, is said to "generate alpha."

Consider the cover of this book—if I added signs along each road, there would be a 'PM' sign before you get to the CIO sign. The portfolio manager role is achieved by excelling at one of the main careers listed in the following pages. You cannot expect to be promoted to portfolio manager until you've succeeded at an analyst role discussed in the coming pages! Consequently, the portfolio manager career is not discussed here beyond being a role you may eventually earn as a promotion.

A Personal Note About Your Analyst Career

An analyst's main role is to view a company or security from the vantage point of whether it is wise to invest in that company. When analyzing a company, you will need to know the company's product, competitive advantage, sales strategy, relationship with suppliers, and details about their current and future competitors. You will need to tie that analysis back to a final conclusion of whether a company or security is overpriced, underpriced, or fairly priced. All of this is known as "fundamental analysis". This analysis extends to non-corporate securities such as real estate and structured bonds.

You will be expected to develop true expertise in what you analyze. That's a lot easier when you have a genuine interest in the subject matter. I am a huge TV and movie buff. I covered those industries as a rating-agency analyst and thoroughly enjoyed my time doing so. In my current job as a buy-side analyst, we hired a junior analyst who had just graduated with an MBA and had previously served in the military. He was a great choice to cover the aerospace and defense sector.

Most of the careers in this bucket are tailor-made for someone who is analytically curious and enjoys putting the pieces of a puzzle together to deliver a logical conclusion. The people who succeed in this career enjoy looking through financial statements and legal documents. They enjoy doing additional due diligence such as visiting a retailer and seeing if sales are in line with expectations or by polling individuals on their buying habits.

The bottom line is that you're going to spend a lot of time at your career. It certainly helps if you enjoy what you're doing!

Analyst #1

BUY-SIDE ANALYST: FIXED INCOME
(Also known as Credit Analyst, Asset Manager, Portfolio Manager, Research Analyst, Institutional Investor)

Career Path	Undergraduate Degree	Advanced Degree	Personality Type	Level of Teamwork
CIO	•Finance •Accounting •Economics	•MBA •CFA •MS in Finance	Introvert	Low

Overview

The fixed income buy-side analyst invests in and manages a portfolio of bonds and loans. Fixed-income investors lend money to corporations, public institutions, and various structured vehicles, such as originators of mortgages or auto loans. They lend with the expectation of being paid recurring quarterly or semi-annual interest, known as the coupon. The principal is returned either in annual payments or, more commonly, as a single "balloon" payment at the loan's maturity. The major employers in this career include mutual funds, insurance companies, general asset managers, and large treasury departments.

A buy-side investor must have a thorough understanding of the corporations receiving loans. This includes its business model, its competitive advantages, new technologies that could pose a threat (think of the iPad disrupting the newspaper industry), pricing power, risk within its supply chain, and customer concentration. The fixed-income investor must be aware of which loans have priority to claim assets in the event of a bankruptcy. A bond at the front of the line with a legal claim to assets typically will be more valuable than one at the back.

Finally, the fixed income buy-side analyst constantly monitors a concept known as "relative value." This compares one investment relative to another to select the most optimal. For example, if bonds in Microsoft yielded only 3%, and bonds in eBay yielded 5%, which would you rather own given that Microsoft is less risky from a business-risk standpoint? Is an incremental 2% (200 basis points) enough to compensate you for eBay's higher default risk?

The same concepts can be applied to non-corporate bonds such as loans to cities or states or to entities building infrastructure projects such as toll roads, stadiums, and airports.

Fixed-Income Buy-Side Analyst: What will I do?

- Manage a portfolio of bonds and recommend buy and sell transactions
- Use financial statements and business models to analyze a bond issuer's ability to pay interest and principal on loans
- Be an expert about the borrower and its prospects to be keenly aware of "cliff risks" – a deterioration in a company's business due to new competitive or technological threats
- Conduct "SWOT" analysis: assess the strengths, weaknesses, opportunities and threats of a business
- Model historical financial results and project future expectations and cash flows
- Be an industry expert—a buy-side investor in technology companies must be knowledgeable about the entire industry
- Work on a trading desk during market hours

Fixed-Income Buy-Side Analyst: What skills and qualities help?

- Enjoy investing; not afraid to take risks and to tolerate market volatility
- Enjoy reading financial statements and financial modeling
- Like puzzles—enjoy putting pieces of information together to find a conclusion

- Good memorization skills to have a thesis on 50 or more companies allowing for quick decisions when a news item arises, such as mergers or earnings news
- Analytically curious—like to perform deep analysis on investment opportunities
- Tolerate being tied to a trading desk and in front of computer screens daily
- Accept very little subjectivity with performance reviews which are performance-based and typically compared to an industry benchmark

Buy-Side Analyst: Fixed Income Examples

- Buy-side analysts use detailed models to judge the prospects of a company. Sebastian is a credit analyst for a global asset manager. He covers the food and beverage industry where he holds corporate bonds from 30 companies. Sebastian updates his Excel models each quarter with the latest financial information. His models include several revenue line items to track sales by brand and by geographic location. He also estimates volume and average price for each brand. He tracks these revenue line items for the past 10 years to monitor trends through different economic cycles. His models also include six cost line items: raw materials, selling, research and development, administrative expenses, interest expense, and income taxes. These models help Sebastian make informed recommendations to buy or sell company bonds. He monitors cash flow generation and other financial information to determine a company's ability to pay interest on its debt commitments. He is watchful for significant risks food and beverage companies face, such as a wave of new, organic products that could alter the competitive landscape.

  Note: This example of a highly detailed financial model is also very relevant to other careers listed in later pages, including sell-side analyst, equity buy-side analyst, hedge fund analyst, and rating agency analyst.

- Buy-side analysts must make data-driven investment decisions. Erin is a fixed-income analyst at ABC Insurance Company (ABC). She spent the past week diving into the financial statements and business model of a company called FIS Global. The work included a deep analysis of the company's balance sheet, income statement, and cash-flow statement. It also incorporated an assessment of the technological risk that FIS's product line of accounting software for banks could be replaced. After the week of due diligence, Erin believed the $100 par value 5% coupon on FIS's 10-year bonds represented a relative value compared to bonds from similar corporations. Erin believed the complexity of FIS's business model discouraged other analysts from tackling a similar deep-dive analysis. Recognizing an opportunity, she recommended to her boss that ABC invest $50 million in FIS. A year later, FIS announced its fourth consecutive quarter of strong earnings. The bonds Erin purchased traded substantially higher at $115, creating a large and welcome gain for ABC.

- Buy-side analysts are judged by their investment decisions. William is a fixed-income investor at ABC Mutual Fund. ABC is very conservative and does not want William to make risky investments. William initially recommended ABC pass on a bond from food distributor Sysco Corporation. Sysco's 10-year bonds were offered at a yield of 3.5%, and the proceeds were earmarked to fund its pending acquisition of competitor US Foods. Several months later, William believed he made a mistake by not purchasing the Sysco bonds. As a result, William recommended to his boss that ABC buy $100 million face value of the 10-year bonds. Unfortunately, the bonds had outperformed the broader market and were now trading at $106 per bond (versus the $100 par price at initial offer). The higher price assumed the acquisition of US Foods would be approved.

    Several months after his purchase, Sysco announced it would terminate its acquisition agreement since the deal was expected to be blocked by the US Federal Trade Commission. The commission feared two very large industry players would create a near monopoly. Unfortunately for William, the bonds had a mandatory redemption feature that required Sysco to redeem all bonds at a price of $101 if the acquisition was terminated. The bonds William bought at $106 had to be resold back to the company at $101, creating a $5 million loss for ABC in only a few months.

- Buy-side analysts must judge the finances of states and cities just as they would companies. Fidelity Investments Municipal Income Fund invests in municipal bond offerings with maturities ranging from less than one year to more than 20 years. The portfolio includes bonds issued by the Illinois Financial Revenue Authority, Miami-Dade County school system in Florida, and the New Jersey Economic Development Authority.

- Buy-side analysts need to make logical arguments for their investment choices. Maureen is an investor for a general asset manager. She is responsible for structured-finance investments such as commercial mortgage-backed securities (CMBS). She recently invested in a 30-year, fully amortizing CMBS that will pay 5% interest. The CMBS is comprised of 52 different properties throughout the southeast and West Coast of the United States, including office buildings in Charlotte, Atlanta, Miami, Seattle, and San Francisco. Maureen likes the geographic diversification of the mortgage pool. She also likes the underlying businesses of the tenants in the properties, which include financial services, pharmaceuticals, and media. The CMBS is structured to have a 2x debt-service coverage ratio (DSCR), which means the cash flows from rental income are two times the amount needed to pay interest and principal amortization. Maureen also likes that the CMBS gives her a first-lien security claim on all underlying property should there be a default.

- Buy-side analysts must be extremely thorough to consider all possible outcomes. Pension Fund XYZ invested $50 million in bonds issued by computer maker Dell. The bonds had a 30-year maturity and were priced to yield 5.4%, which XYZ thought was a great investment. Three years later, Dell's founder, Michael Dell, decided to take the company back to being a private entity for $25 billion. To finance the transaction, he would offer new bank loans and bonds security on all assets of the company. When the main analyst for XYZ checked the indentures (legal documents) for their 5.4% bonds, he was shocked to learn that there was no protection against Dell granting security on assets for new debt, thereby subordinating XYZ's bonds. As a result, the 5.4% bonds became more risky and quickly traded down to $70 (versus $100 par) to yield 7.7%. This resulted in a $15 million decline in bond value for XYZ.

Analyst #1a

BUY-SIDE ANALYST: EQUITY

(Also known as Asset Manager, Portfolio Manager, Research Analyst, Institutional Investor)

Career Path	Undergraduate Degree	Advanced Degree	Personality Type	Level of Teamwork
CIO	•Finance •Accounting •Economics	•MBA •CFA •MS in Finance	Introvert	Low

Overview

The equity buy-side analyst role is very similar to the fixed income buy-side career. The big difference is that the career focuses on the common stock of public companies rather than the debt of those entities. A fixed-income investor can also lend to private companies whereas the buy-side equity investor is limited to *public* equity. (Private company investing is a different category and is covered later in this book in the "Private Equity" and "Venture Capital" sections.) The major employers in this career include mutual funds and general asset managers.

From an analytical standpoint, the equity and fixed-income roles are similar but the sensitivity involved in an equity investment is far greater than with a bond. If Microsoft has $100 billion in cash and only $50 billion in debt while generating more than $20 billion a year in cash flow, it is a pretty safe assumption that a Microsoft bond will not react if the company misses its earnings per share (EPS) target by a few cents in a quarterly earnings report. But the company's stock price likely would be impacted negatively if the company announced $2.60 of earnings per share when analysts had expected $2.70. Consequently, an equity buy-side investor typically digs deeper into the quarterly operations of a company: Was there a delay in the release of a new product? Was there a disruption in the supply chain? Was the company able to pass through a larger price increase than previously expected?

Was demand for its product greater than anticipated? All these factors could be short-term in nature and not represent a major shift in the company's strategic positioning. But they matter to the equity investor because they could represent buying or selling opportunities. These smaller nuances are even more important to hedge-fund analysts (a role that is discussed later).

Given the higher sensitivity issues, an equity analyst typically covers fewer companies or industries than a fixed-income analyst. A fixed-income analyst might cover multiple sectors such as technology, media, and retail while an equity analyst will typically cover only one of those sectors. Further, the equity analyst could focus on a specific mandate, such as investing in only growth companies or companies that pay dividends or companies with market capitalizations of less than $1 billion.

Beyond these differences, the fundamental job of equity analysts is very similar to fixed-income analysts: both must thoroughly understand the company they invest in—its business model, its competitive advantages, new technologies that provide an opportunity or pose a threat, pricing power, customer concentration, and many other factors.

Buy-Side Equity Analyst: What will I do?

- Manage portfolios of public stocks and recommend buy and sell transactions
- Analyze company growth and dividend prospects and long-term viability
- Develop expertise about a company and be keenly aware of "cliff risks" – significant threats to a company such as technological change or new competition
- Conduct "SWOT" analysis: assess the strengths, weaknesses, opportunities, and threats of a company
- Model historical financial results and project future expectations and cash flows
- Build expertise about an industry's outlook
- Work on a trading desk during market hours

Buy-Side Equity Analyst: What skills and qualities help?

- Comfortable working with numbers and math
- Enjoy investing– willing to take risks and tolerate market volatility
- Like financial modeling and creating projections and sensitivity scenarios
- Enjoy reading financial statements
- Like puzzles—enjoy putting pieces of information together to find a final conclusion
- Good memorization skills to have a thesis on 25 or more companies to allow for quick decisions when material news arises such as mergers, acquisitions, earnings, or management changes
- Analytically curious to perform deep-dive analysis on investment opportunities
- Accept very little subjectivity with performance reviews which are performance-based and compared to an industry benchmark

Buy-Side Analyst: Equity Examples

- Fidelity Investments manages more than 1,000 US equity mutual funds. The funds have specializations such as large-capitalization income, large-capitalization growth, large-cap defensive, and various value funds. The company's large-cap growth fund includes Apple and Microsoft as two of its biggest holdings, indicating that the buy-side analyst covering the technology sector favorably views the growth prospects of both companies.
- Jeannie is a buy-side equity analyst at XYZ Asset Management focusing on growth companies. She bought one million shares of Nvidia Corporation stock at $60 per share. Nvidia held a dominant position in making semiconductor graphic chips for video games and Jeannie believed the $60 per share fully reflected that business. Based on significant due diligence, she recognized that the company's products could also be used in newer technologies, such as machine learning and automated vehicles. Her belief was based on careful analysis as she attended technology conferences and heard product managers discuss breakthroughs

that bypassed older technology components. Jeannie was correct—Nvidia announced strong growth in the new businesses, resulting in the stock price tripling to $180 per share over a 12-month period.

- Jeannie's colleague Faye at XYZ Asset Manager focuses on value stocks. She has been analyzing a company called TE Connectivity (TE) that makes wires and connectors for electronics and automobiles. Faye believes the company's stock represents a good value relative to other investment opportunities. At its current price of $60 per share, the company's price-to-earnings ratio (P/E) is only 14x. The stocks of close competitors trade at 20x. After much due diligence, Faye attributes this discrepancy to TE's overexposure to the volatile automobile industry. Faye agrees that the US automotive market can be cyclical and susceptible to economic downturns but she believes the international automotive market, which is a far bigger part of TE's business, should enjoy another decade of strong growth. These views, along with TE's high dividend yield and stability of its nonautomotive business, lead Faye to recommend to her boss that XYZ purchase 5 million shares of TE.

- Many of the world's largest asset managers, such as Fidelity, State Street, and Franklin Templeton, will not only manage money for their retail mutual-fund clients but also manage smaller portfolios for private clients. A portion of these private clients are detailed in the Third-Party Management career.

- Gary is a buy-side equity analyst for a major mutual fund that focuses on growth investments. He follows more than 30 companies across the pharmaceutical sector. Gary covers all 30 companies even though his fund invests in only 20 of them. He covers the additional 10 in case a good buying opportunity arises if the market overreacts to negative news. Gary keeps detailed financial models of all 30 companies, updating historical results with each quarterly earnings release. He also updates future projections of revenues, expenses, and cash flows to prepare for a buying opportunity.

Analyst #1b

HEDGE FUND ANALYST

(Also known as Asset Manager, Portfolio Manager, Distressed Investor, Special-Situation Analyst, Long-Short Analyst, Arbitrage Analyst, Activist Investor, Institutional Investor)

Career Path	Undergraduate Degree	Advanced Degree	Personality Type	Level of Teamwork
CIO	•Finance •Economics •Math/Statistics •Various sciences	•MBA •CFA •MBA-JD	Introvert	Low

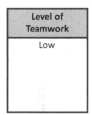

Overview

A hedge-fund analyst combines the buy-side fixed-income and buy-side equity roles discussed earlier. These analysts usually have more freedom to invest in any part of a company's capital structure—recall all the terms discussed earlier in this chapter including common stock, preferred stock, subordinated bonds, unsecured bonds, secured bonds, and derivatives. None of these instruments is off limits to a hedge-fund analyst. An analyst can also combine fundamental analysis, using financial statements and valuations, with what is referred to as technical indicators which rely on quantitative and computer-driven models that factor in trends, correlations, and the concept of reversion-to-the-mean. Finally, a hedge fund analyst can go "long" a security (bet its value will increase) or "short" a security (bet its value will decline).

Traditional buy-side analysts typically take a long-term view of their investments but hedge funds can adopt a very short-term view. This includes very specific mandates, such as "special situations," where an analyst makes an investment decision based on a speculated outcome regarding potential mergers and acquisitions, litigation, or product performance. Consequently, a single investment can sometimes make – or break – an entire year for a hedge-fund analyst.

Hedge Fund Analyst: What will I do?

- Perform duties discussed earlier in the buy-side analyst sections but typically with shorter-term views
- Invest in any part of a company's capital structure and bet that an investment's value will go higher (long) or lower (short)
- Find opportunities in bankruptcy situations by examining legal structures to identify claims on assets and subordination
- Model historical financial results and project future expectations and cash flows
- Develop expertise in specific industries
- Perform advanced financial-statement analysis and understand quantitative analysis

Hedge Fund Analyst: What skills and qualities help?

- Enjoy modeling financial projections, sensitivity scenarios, and sometimes technical trading
- Extremely quick thinker under pressure
- Tolerant of potentially less job security
- Enjoy investing and not intimidated by market volatility and risk taking
- Analytically curious to perform deep analysis for specific micro data
- Enjoy completing puzzles by assembling pieces of information to find a final conclusion
- Accept very little subjectivity with performance reviews which are performance-based compared to an industry benchmark

Hedge Fund Analyst Examples

- Hedge fund analysts must make controversial decisions that might backfire. Pershing Square Capital shorted (bet against) hundreds of millions of dollars' worth of Herbalife stock and created a campaign stating that the company was an illegal pyramid scheme. The campaign included a 340-page slide deck presented to investors at an industry conference, detailing Herbalife's products, pricing, recruiting, and commission practices. The stock traded in the low $30 per-share range at the time. Other investors disputed Pershing's assessment and bet the stock would rise. Herbalife was eventually investigated by the Federal Trade Commission, which assessed a $200 million fine but the agency did not label Herbalife a pyramid scheme. Herbalife's stock rose during the four years following Pershing's initial bet against the company which resulted in significant losses for Pershing.

- Hedge fund analysts must recognize unusual opportunities. According to the *Wall Street Journal*, hedge funds Elliott Management and Bracebridge Capital made significant returns on Argentinian bonds they had purchased years earlier. Argentina announced it had reached a deal to pay $4.65 billion to four hedge funds, including Elliot and Bracebridge, to settle claims on sovereign debt from a 2001 default on more than $80 billion. Elliott was expected to make a return of nearly 400% on principal, while Bracebridge was expected to make a return of more than 950%, or $1.1 billion, on $120 million in principal. The agreement ended a 15-year saga that prevented Argentina from borrowing in the global market. The original bonds were issued before Argentina stumbled into serious economic problems and included terms that increased their value when interest rates soared (the interest rate on the bonds was "floating" so increased when Argentina experienced historic inflation).

- Lori is a hedge-fund analyst at XYZ Management. She has followed semiconductor company Advanced Micro Devices (AMD) for several years. AMD competes against other semiconductor stalwarts such as Intel and Nvidia and had a multi-year string of poor results. Performance was so bad that AMD's stock price traded as low as $2 per share, and its bonds due in 2019 were trading at just 60 cents on the dollar. After examining the company's capital structure, Lori felt the 2019 bonds offered compelling value. She believed that despite poor performance, the company's position as a secondary semiconductor supplier to PC makers had a modest value. More importantly, she believed its intellectual property in its graphic processor unit (GPU) business was worth more than the company's combined $2 billion in debt. After performing further due diligence, Lori confirmed her initial thoughts—AMD had a good competitive position in the GPU market and growth expectations in the coming years.

Lori bought $20 million of the AMD's 6.75% 2019 bonds at $62 per bond which yielded nearly 11%. Lori believed that if AMD went into bankruptcy, the recovery value would be $100 per bond. She also predicted other investors would soon recognize AMD's value and be willing to refinance the 2019 bonds. Six months after Lori's investment, AMD closed a new convertible-bond deal, resulting in Lori's bonds being redeemed at $109 per bond. The $9 over par represented an early pre-payment premium. XYZ pocketed a 75% gain worth more than $9 million on the transaction.

- Clem worked in the special-situations group of ABC Hedge Fund. His team's mission was to discover special events such as a merger, litigation, or a product hit or miss that could cause a substantial price swing in a company's stock or bonds. Clem had viewed the food and beverage industry as ripe for change, as more people preferred healthier organic foods. He believed the company Annie's was a perfect candidate to be acquired by a more established food company since it offered popular organic snack and dinner items. Clem noticed that Annie's stock had declined from $45 per share to $30 a share even though his overall thesis about consumer desire for healthier food remained intact. Clem purchased $10 million of Annie's stock, believing the recent sell-off made it even more attractive to an acquirer. Shortly after Clem's purchase, the food conglomerate General Mills offered to acquire Annie's at $46 per share, netting Clem and ABC a return of more than 50% in two weeks.

- Elizabeth also worked for ABC Hedge Fund. She thought owning Amazon stock was a sure thing given the company's continued growth in traditional retail and its success in its Web services business. In fact, the only thing Elizabeth worried about regarding Amazon was its correlation to the technology sector. After assessing the overall correlation between the stock and the technology index, Elizabeth constructed a "pair-trade" that went long $10 million of Amazon stock while also buying $500,000 of long-dated in-the-money put options on the QQQ Technology Index. This allowed Elizabeth to bet that Amazon's value would increase but it also provided some hedge protection in case the company's stock declined due to an industry-wide technology sector sell-off.

- The term "activist investor" can be applied to many types of asset managers although the hedge fund career is the most applicable in this book. An activist investor is someone who buys an ownership stake in a *public* company with the intention of taking an active role in the overall operational and financial strategies. Methods vary greatly for activist investors but their common end goal is to increase a company's value.

    - One example was Carl Icahn pushing eBay to separate out its PayPal business. Icahn cited a lack of synergy between the two businesses. He spotted more opportunity for growth for both as stand-alone entities. A conglomerate owning multiple businesses may sometimes be referred to as a "value trap" if investors don't fully value each business appropriately.
    - Another example was hedge fund Pershing Square taking an equity stake in Canadian Pacific Railway (CP). Pershing changed CP's management team by bringing in people from its largest competitor Canadian National Railway (CN). Pershing believed that CP had a similar footprint to CN but was valued at a substantial discount due to weaker operations such as slower train speed and longer wait times at stations.

        The end result for both Icahn and Pershing in these examples was a substantial increase in their stakes' values. Other activist strategies include prompting management for more aggressive debt-financed dividends or stock repurchases and splitting up real estate ownership from an operating business (Macy's sold prime real estate in New York and San

Francisco and entered into a rent agreement for the land instead).

The private equity career discussed later has many similarities as the activist investor. The biggest difference is the size of the ownership in a company. While an activist investor can typically seek to make changes with a small ownership stake in a public company, private equity typically looks to take over 100% of a company and remove it from public markets. Successful activist investor Trian Partners adopted the motto: "Trian is a *highly engaged shareowner,* bringing a private equity mindset to the public markets".

One final thought: what is on the other side of the proposals an activist investor might push for? A lot of extra work and analysis for the CEO, CFO, finance, investor relations, and treasury teams of the target!

Analyst #2

ECONOMIST/STRATEGIST

Career Path	Undergraduate Degree	Advanced Degree	Personality Type	Level of Teamwork
•CIO (buy-side) •MD/Partner (sell-side)	•Economics •International studies •Math/Statistics	•MBA •CFA •MA/PhD Economics	Extrovert	Medium

Overview

The economist, who is also known as a strategist at some companies, takes a bird's-eye view on asset management by folding in global economic data and events. At the most basic level, there are two economist roles:

a) <u>Buy-side Economist</u>: reporting to the chief investment officer (CIO) of an asset manager
b) <u>Sell-side Economist</u>: part of an investment bank or advisory firm

This role tracks all US and international macro data, such as gross domestic product (GDP), inflation, employment, retail sales, and industrial production. The economist ties that back to an outlook on equity markets, interest rates, commodities and currencies. This prognostication is used for portfolio construction to determine allocation of cash, equities, corporate bonds, municipal bonds, structured securities, real estate, and derivatives. While the previously discussed buy-side analysts are responsible for the micro details of a company, referred to as unique or "unsystematic risk," the economist is responsible for the "systematic" or market risk.

It should be noted that a company's economist team usually includes quantitative experts. These are people who run simulations to project different outcomes using different scenarios, such as how changing employment projections impacts GDP forecasts. These quantitative experts play a key role in some economist groups.

Economist/Strategist: What will I do?

- Track all weekly, monthly, and quarterly macro information flows from global government sources such as GDP, consumer price index (CPI), employment, and interest rates
- Predict how global data will impact the performance of equity markets, interest rates (for bond markets), currencies, and commodities
- Recommend asset-allocation strategies and portfolio weightings, such as whether it will be more favorable to emphasize equities, US bonds, emerging markets, or other securities
- Monitor global events to interpret the forces causing those events
- For specialized groups at sell-side investment banks, cover the non-corporate markets such as municipals, mortgage-backed securities, and asset-backed securities

Economist/Strategist: What skills and qualities help?

- Like working with high-level government data
- Enjoy interpreting geographic and political changes and foreign policy
- Enjoy predicting how foreign policy changes in one region can impact other regions
- Enjoy advising and public speaking
- Enjoy writing—many economists disseminate their views through research reports
- Analytically curious
- Ability to tolerate market volatility

- Sell-side economists must be willing to travel to meet clients seeking views on regional macro analyses

Economist/Strategist Examples

- Kimberly is a buy-side fixed-income analyst covering the industrial and chemical sectors at a major mutual fund. Her coverage includes companies such as Monsanto and Caterpillar, which have significant exposure to Brazil and other South American countries. Kimberly believes the fundamentals of these companies are rock solid given their market share and technological leadership. But she considers the valuations of their bonds to be a little high. Gary is the buy-side economist/strategist at the same mutual fund. He suggests Latin America is headed for a recession given recent gross domestic product and consumer-price data. As a result, the CIO reduces the mutual fund company's investments in several companies with exposure to South America (including Caterpillar and Monsanto) until Gary decides the region is in a recovery phase.
- The sell-side economic team for ABC Bank spends two-thirds of its time traveling the country meeting with clients, participating in panel discussions, and making conference calls. The team advises clients on its global economic forecast for various geographic regions, including the United States, South America, the Eurozone, China, Australia, and Japan. As part of its presentations, the team details its forecasts for each region's gross domestic product, employment data, currency-exchange rates, interest rates, and overall political and regulatory expectations. Clients use these forecasts to determine portfolio allocation for asset classes and geographic regions.
- The chief economist for Deutsche Bank stated, during a CNBC TV interview, that he believed the odds of a US recession were 40%. He believed the US consumer was healthy due to record-low

energy costs. But he believed a confluence of factors such as low gross domestic product growth, export weakness due to a strong US dollar, soft business spending, and global economic weakness all threatened to outweigh the strength of US consumer spending.

- ABC Bank's sell-side economic team advised clients to hedge their exposure to the British pound over the next two years by purchasing forward contracts that allowed them to purchase pounds for $1.65. The team expected exchange rates to become more expensive for US clients given their projections on interest rates and the gross domestic product for the two countries. Unfortunately, the economic team failed to factor in the low-probability chances around "Brexit," a vote by Britain to leave the European Union. A subsequent sell-off of the pound dropped the currency's value to $1.25. The miscalculation cost the company's clients because they bought pounds at a $1.65 rate rather than waiting for a decline to $1.25.
- Sell-side strategists at XYZ Bank publish weekly reports on the mortgage-backed security market. The reports are distributed to buy-side and hedge fund clients and provide high-level macro data around security performance. The reports also have topical discussions about interest rate and regulatory environments, and how those issues could impact the value of mortgage-backed securities.

Analyst #3

SELL-SIDE ANALYST (EQUITY AND FIXED INCOME)
(Also known as Research Analyst, Desk Analyst, Credit Analyst [Fixed Income])

Career Path	Undergraduate Degree	Advanced Degree	Personality Type	Level of Teamwork
•MD/Partner •CIO (indirect, via move to buy-side)	•Finance •Accounting •Various sciences	•MBA •CFA •CPA	Extrovert	Low

Overview

If you have ever watched one of the television business channels, you've probably seen a sell-side analyst. These are the men and women working for large banks or boutique companies who discuss the stocks they like and dislike. Economists/strategists are also common guests on business television. Beyond the glamorous TV opportunities, the sell-side analyst role is extremely difficult. There are separate sell-side analysts for both the equity and fixed-income markets.

a) Equity Sell-Side: The equity sell-side role is responsible for covering all companies within a specific subsector and placing price estimates on their stocks. Sell-side clients typically are buy-side and hedge-fund analysts. While a typical buy-side analyst may cover a larger sector such as technology, the equity sell-side analyst is more specialized and may focus only on semiconductors or software.

The equity sell-side analyst keeps extremely detailed models on all companies covered with projections based on highly detailed assumptions around operations such as volume and pricing. An Apple analyst projects volumes and prices of the iPhone and iPad for every region in the world. The analyst also needs to spot trends that may pose new threats and be aware of economic data that could indicate a recession.

An equity sell-side analyst is the main participant in quarterly and annual earnings calls of public corporations. Those calls will typically include a company's chief executive and financial officers and investor-relations official answering questions from the sell-side analysts covering that stock.

An equity sell-side analyst spends much time on the road visiting buy-side and hedge fund clients, as well as meeting with management teams.

Interestingly, some sell-side analysts have technical backgrounds. Wells Fargo technology sell-side analyst David Wong, for example, has undergraduate, graduate, and PhD degrees in electrical engineering as well as being a Chartered Financial Analyst (CFA).

b) Fixed-Income Sell-Side: The fixed-income sell-side analyst role is similar to the equity role with two important differences: (1) The analyst covers company bonds rather than stocks, and (2) The analyst typically covers a broader range of sectors and subsectors (e.g., technology, media, and retail). The reason for the wider coverage is that not all companies have outstanding bonds. Whereas the equity sell-side analyst focuses on stock-price estimates, the fixed-income sell-side analyst focuses on bond prices and yields and relative value (discussed in the "Buy-Side: Fixed Income" section). Fixed-income sell-side analysts that cover noncorporate markets such as structured finance and municipals are discussed in the Economist/Strategist section.

Sell-side analysts are expected to publish a large volume of research. This includes specific company reports, as well as larger "thought pieces" that may discuss broad industry or secular trends. These thought pieces can be hundreds of pages and cover broad topical issues such as trends in TV viewing habits, technology buying patterns, or electric vehicles, to name a few.

The sell-side analyst also plays a crucial syndicate role within an investment bank's capital markets operations. In this capacity, the sell-side analyst will be the first to meet with a company seeking to access the capital markets. Consider a company that wants to raise a $500 million bond deal. The sell-side analyst will meet with the company's management to understand its business and risks. The sell-side analyst is then responsible for educating colleagues in investment banking, trading, and institutional sales (all three of these roles are discussed in "Bucket #3: Matchmakers").

Under the sell-side business model at large banks, research is generally free to buy-side and hedge-fund investors. The expectation is that the sell-side research will generate goodwill when the investors place buy and sell orders with traders. This lack of a clear revenue stream makes the sell-side business volatile during recessionary times, when banks seek to cut employment without materially impacting their trading business. This has also resulted in some banks eliminating the publishing aspects of their sell-side analysts in favor of keeping their work as an internal resource for their traders. This role is known as a "desk analyst".

Sell-Side Analyst: What will I do?

- Write and disseminate research explaining what stocks and bonds to buy, sell, or hold
- Work closely with the trading desk and traders, recommending what stocks and bonds to buy, sell, or hold (desk analyst)
- Maintain detailed models and projections. For equity sell-side, this includes stock price conclusions based on net present value of future cash flows or on multiples of similar businesses
- Analyze a company's management efficiency by calculating return on investment, return on equity, and other measures to compare a company's performance versus competitors
- Participate in question and answer sessions during earnings calls and analysts events
- Develop an understanding of a company's product and overall strategy
- Meet with investors to offer a thesis on performance, expectations, and overall pricing
- Compete and market for *Institutional Investor* ranking, where buy-side investors rank their favorite sell-side analysts

Sell-Side Analyst: What skills and qualities help?

- Enjoy writing, including long, detailed reports
- Willing to work very long hours to meet publishing deadlines
- Analytically curious to perform deep analysis for very specific micro data
- Enjoy completing puzzles by assembling pieces of information to find a final conclusion
- Enjoy reading financial statements
- Like creating financial models, projections, and sensitivity scenarios
- Like to travel to meet with buy-side clients
- Ability to withstand the volatility of the stock and bond markets
- Enjoy public speaking
- Want to live in a major financial center such as New York, London, and Hong Kong

Sell-Side Analyst Examples

- Jim is an equity sell-side analyst at ABC Bank, responsible for covering 20 different companies in the hotel sector. Each quarter, Jim updates his models with the latest financial information. His detailed models include revenue line items for occupancy, room rates, food services, and general merchandise. He tracks each line item for the past 10 years to monitor trends through different economic cycles. He also uses these line items as the basis for each company's five-year projections. His models also include six different cost line items: rent expense, cost of food and merchandise, hotel personnel salaries, administrative expenses, interest expense, and income taxes. The revenue and cost figures are netted to determine each company's after-tax net income.

  These detailed models form the basis for Jim's buy and sell recommendations and how he determines the valuations of companies he covers. He discounts back his net income projections to arrive at a per-share value. He uses his models across the 20 companies he covers to compare trends and overall performance.

This example is similar to one provided in the buy-side fixed income section. This example is equally relevant for the buy-side equity and hedge fund analyst. The ability to use models to understand a company's financial standing is the most fundamental function of all these roles.

- Jim has a "buy" rating on ABC Hotels Inc. He arrived at this buy recommendation through his discounted cash flow model. Specifically, ABC has $100 million in revenue and $80 million in costs, for an after-tax profit of $20 million. Jim believes ABC can grow revenues 12% per year over the next 5 years by increasing room rates. Since this price increase is not accompanied by any incremental costs, Jim expects the price increase to fall directly to the bottom line. This results in the $20 million of after-tax profit growing to nearly $100 million by the end of year 5. Jim discounts back these five years of cash flows at ABC's weighted average cost of capital (WACC) of 5%. He uses a terminal multiple of 10x on the year 5 cash flow and discounts that value back at the same WACC. This results in a total value of nearly $1 billion for ABC. When dividing the $1 billion value by the 10 million shares outstanding, Jim concludes that the stock should be trading at $100 per share versus the current price of $60 per share. Jim immediately publishes a research report for his clients announcing his increase in ABC's price target.
- In an interview with CNBC, an equity sell-side analyst from Nomura Securities kept his "buy" rating on Netflix but lowered his overall price target from $125 per share to $115 per share. The change was due to his expectations for a slowdown in international subscriber growth, especially in Japan and Southern Europe. The $115 price target still represented a 20% increase from that day's trading price.
- Kelly is a sell-side fixed-income analyst covering the pharmaceutical industry. She is following a $10 billion proposed acquisition

of ABC, a manufacturer of off-patent medicine, by XYZ, a leading developer of new pharmaceutical medicine that relies on the exclusivity periods provided by patent protections. XYZ also has a sizeable off-patent business. The equity markets are pricing in a 70% chance the merger will receive regulatory approval.

ABC had $500 million of high-yield bonds outstanding when the merger was announced. Prior to the announcement, the bonds were trading at $100 par for a 6% yield. XYZ is a strong investment-grade entity and its bonds trade at $100 par for a yield of 3%. XYZ has stated it plans to finance the acquisition entirely with debt. That move could risk having its high credit rating fall to the lower end of investment grade.

Immediately after the announcement, ABC's bonds traded up to $120 for a yield of 3.5%. XYZ's bonds had an opposite move: they traded down to $95, to also arrive at a 3.5% yield. Kelly believed the bond market was essentially factoring in a 100% chance of the deal going through, overlooking the regulatory hurdles the proposed deal faces. She strongly believed ABC's bonds had increased in value too aggressively considering the downside risk of the merger being blocked. She thought investors should sell into the initial announcement and take their profits. She issued a report the next day putting a "sell" recommendation on ABC's bonds. Six months later, the merger did not gain regulatory approval. Both bonds traded closer to their $100 par value again, leaving investors who heeded Kelly's advice with a huge profit.

- Ava is a sell-side analyst for ABC Bank, located in New York City. She covers the retail and consumer products sectors and has "sell" ratings on many companies, including Macy's, Nordstrom, and Hasbro. Each year between Thanksgiving and Christmas, she makes dozens of visits to the largest malls in the New York—New Jersey—Connecticut area to do "channel checks" where she sees how foot traffic compares to prior years and how that corresponds to earnings estimates. Her "sell" recommendations take into account the anecdotal evidence she notices during her checks that reveal how foot traffic continues to decrease. She believes this is a result of increased competitive online outlets such as Amazon.com.

Analyst #4

PRIVATE-EQUITY ANALYST
(Also known as Asset Manager, Distressed Investor, Activist Investor, Merchant Banker)

Career Path	Undergraduate Degree	Advanced Degree	Personality Type	Level of Teamwork
MD/Partner	•Finance •Strategy •Economics •Operations Mgmt.	•MBA •CFA •MBA JD	Varies	Medium

Overview

Private-equity firms are turnaround specialists. They acquire public companies and take them private or acquire private companies and keep them private. Their objective is to purchase a company that they perceive as poorly managed, hold it privately while out of the public eye, and improve operations. They then hope to resell the entity at a higher price. Private equity firms use debt to finance the majority of a purchase, magnifying the returns on their equity investment. This is referred to as a Leveraged Buyout or LBO.

A home flipper serves as a good comparison to illustrate private equity. A flipper purchases a fixer-upper, renovates it, installs new appliances, and then resells it to buyers seeking an attractive, move-in-ready home.

While it is easy to see how renovations increase the value of a home, methods used in the corporate world may not be as simple. Private equity typically focuses on three areas:

1) **Cost Cuts:** The easiest way for private equity to increase a company's cash flow is to remove unnecessary expenses. Are there layers of middle management to eliminate? Can suppliers be consolidated to gain lower prices? Can manufacturing be moved to lower-cost regions, such as Mexico or China? Can office space

be reduced? Is the weekly, catered sushi staff lunch necessary? Private-equity firms are pros at analyzing a company's cost structure to eliminate anything not mission critical.

2) **Untapped Revenue Opportunities:** A more difficult way for private equity to improve a company's cash flow is to increase its revenue base. This can be done through methods such as cross-selling – getting existing customers to buy additional products, finding entirely new customers, or improving operations to gain market share through customer loyalty.

3) **Asset Sales:** The last area for private equity to generate returns is the sale of noncore assets or businesses. Private equity typically purchases companies that have assets that can be separated and sold without materially impacting overall cash flow or core business operations. These assets may be undervalued by the seller. This is known as a "value trap" where a group of combined businesses don't receive the sum of the valuation they would warrant as separate companies.

Making cost cuts and finding new revenue improve overall cash flow which makes a company more attractive to buyers.

Consider a company that private equity acquires at a 10x cash-flow multiple. In other words, private equity pays $1 billion for a company generating $100 million of annual cash flow. If through cost cuts and new revenue generation, private equity doubles the company's cash flow to $200 million per year that same 10x multiple raises the company's value to $2 billion—a $1 billion or 100% return before tax on the original purchase price. What's more, private equity typically finances the initial $1 billion purchase price with only $200 million equity (the other $800 million is borrowed). By applying that same $1 billion return on $200 million equity investment you get a 500% return! It's important to note that the debt borrowed is a risky proposition. The interest expense on that debt creates an additional financial obstacle in the path to increasing cash flow. It also becomes a major problem if the cost cuts or revenue increases are not achieved. Private equity closely considers those issues when calculating a realistic net gain to target.

The third area—asset sales—typically results in private equity paying a quick dividend to its shareholders or using the proceeds to reduce the acquired company's debt load.

Think about a private-equity firm that acquires a food retailer under the same assumptions used above—the food retailer generates $100 million of cash flows and private equity pays $1 billion for the company (financed 80% with debt). Years earlier, the food retailer wanted to know more about its customers so it developed a proprietary loyalty-card technology that tracked purchase habits and improved inventory planning. The technology was very valuable but the food retailer kept it solely for internal use so it didn't generate revenue for the company. In fact, it cost the company money to maintain it.

After private equity acquired the food retailer, it decided to sell that proprietary technology to a Silicon Valley company which could market the software to other retailers. Based on the prospects, the private-equity firm believed the technology could generate $25 million of annual cash flow in the future and believed the technology's growth prospects would command a high multiple—20x—to a purchaser. That means a private-equity firm could sell that technology to a Silicon Valley firm for $500 million—enough to earn 250% on its initial $200 million equity investment before even touching the core business!

These examples are oversimplified and obviously easier said than done. But they illustrate essentially how private-equity companies consider potential investments.

Be aware that private-equity firms do not invest solely in under-managed corporations. They also invest in assets of all types, such as depressed real estate and infrastructure. In addition, private equity's investment horizon varies greatly but can generally be thought of as somewhere between two and five years. Firms want to sell to monetize their investments as soon as possible and move on to the next "fixer-upper."

Private Equity Analyst: What will I do?

- Invest money in *private* assets or take public companies private
- Turn around the operations of underperforming companies
- Develop the ability to understand the existing cost structure of a company and compare it to other industry participants to find cost reductions
- Understand business operations and customer and competitor trends to creatively access new revenue streams
- Conduct "SWOT" analysis: assess the strengths, weaknesses, opportunities, and threats of a potential investment
- Create exit strategies that require a good understanding for the prospects of an initial public offering (IPO) or a strategic buyer once operations are improved
- Thoroughly analyze financial statements and perform due diligence
- Model sensitivity scenarios revolving around synergy levels, exit strategies, and asset sales

Private Equity Analyst: What skill and qualities help?

- A cost-cutting focus
- Willingness to take risks
- Enjoy negotiating
- Analytically curious
- Creative thinker to develop business strategy and financing packages
- A strong understanding of capital markets and the ability to raise capital from innovative sources

- Not afraid to take control of a company and make bold changes
- Strong modeling capabilities

Private Equity Analyst Examples

- Private-equity firm Apollo Global Management announced its acquisition of home-security company The ADT Corporation for about $7 billion. At the time, ADT was the clear market-share industry leader with more than a 20% share. Apollo already owned another top five company, Protection1. Apollo's acquisition's rationale was to merge ADT with Protection1 to consolidate operations and save money on corporate overhead such as legal, accounting, treasury and back-office operations including accounts receivable, accounts payable, customer service, and monitoring facilities. The purchase would also eliminate ADT expenses associated with being a public company such as the cost of preparing Security and Exchange Commission public filings.
- Private-equity firm Silver Lake Investments joined Michael Dell in 2013 to acquire and take private Dell Computers. Dell specialized in supplying PCs and servers to small- and medium-sized businesses. Three years after going private, Dell and Silver Lake acquired fellow technology company EMC Corp. for a staggering $67 billion. EMC was a leader in data-center storage and was especially dominant with large and global-sized companies. In addition to overhead-cost reductions, the private-equity group believed it could gain revenue synergies. It aimed to have Dell's sales force sell EMC storage products to small and medium-sized business while EMC's sales force would sell Dell servers to larger global enterprises. To finance a portion of the $67 billion price tag, Dell sold nearly $8 billion worth of noncore businesses, including EMC's Enterprise Content Division, which had no synergies with the storage, PC, or server businesses.
- Private-equity firm Blackstone Group took Hilton Hotels private in 2007 for approximately $26 billion. In addition to its namesake brand, Hilton owned the Hampton Inn, Embassy Suites,

and DoubleTree brands. Blackstone's plan was to become more aggressive with a "capital light" strategy: a focus on higher-margin franchise agreements where they licensed to franchisees various brands, booking systems, and loyalty-points programs. Under this strategy, Hilton would collect a fee on room revenue from the franchisees and avoid costly overhead tied to building and owning properties.

Blackstone eventually exited most of its investment through an initial public offering (IPO) of Hilton. The path to the IPO, however, was not easy. The company bought Hilton when stock markets were peaking. Blackstone invested nearly $6 billion of its own money and layered on $20 billion of debt just before the financial crisis hit. The financial crisis of 2008 and 2009 resulted in a severe reduction in travel that negatively impacted Hilton's revenues and cash flows. Hilton faced a challenge to pay interest on its massive debt and eventually had to restructure its terms with lenders to gain some financial flexibility. Despite the unexpected financial hurdles, many media outlets estimated that Blackstone earned a profit on its investment despite the tumultuous ride.

Analyst #5

VENTURE CAPITALIST

Career Path	Undergraduate Degree	Advanced Degree	Personality Type	Level of Teamwork
MD/Partner	•Finance •Strategy •Various other	•MBA •MBA-JD	Varies	Medium

Overview

Unlike private-equity firms that invest in existing struggling or under-performing companies, venture capitalists (VCs) invest in *ideas* and *new companies*, also known as start-ups.

Most people think of Silicon Valley as the mecca of VCs, but they can be found in every industry. Think of all the new organic and healthy food and beverage products on your local supermarket's shelves. Many were funded by VCs. The medical industry also has a large VC presence. Young companies face many years of expensive research and development costs before generating any substantive cash flows so require multiple rounds of capital-raising. This makes the VC industry very risky. Many investments never develop into a sustainable business.

The primary job of a VC analyst is to understand industry trends and determine how an incumbent's position can be defeated through a better product or service. In addition to investment funds, VCs provide business-advisory and financial-planning services to start-up companies that may lack business expertise. This puts the VC in the important position of "steering from behind" and advising on business strategy, marketing, and capital decision making – many of the things discussed in "Bucket #1: Practitioner."

Like private-equity analysts, VCs need an exit strategy for their investments. These typically come in two forms: an initial public offering that turns a private company public or a sale of the company to a larger strategic buyer. Keeping a company private under VC ownership has become more common but that is a relatively recent phenomenon. VCs typically are not interested in owning a completely private company for an extended time. They prefer to monetize their investments and move to the next idea.

It's worth noting that unlike private equity firms, VCs use equity to finance their investments rather than debt.

Venture Capitalist: What will I do?

- Invest in ideas and start-up companies
- Understand industry trends and customer preferences and motivations
- Predict future demand shifts
- Perform "SWOT" analysis: assess the strengths, weaknesses, opportunities, and threats of a potential start-up or investment idea
- Incubate a start-up and serve as a financial, operational, and strategic advisor for everything from sales strategies to capital-raising activities
- Develop exit strategies—understand the initial public offering market and how VC-backed companies may fit into larger incumbent companies

Venture Capitalist: What skills and qualities help?

- Analytically curious
- Strategic thinker
- Interested in consumer trends, habits, and preferences
- Have knowledge of the industry a portfolio company operates in such as technology, medicine, alternative energy, and food and beverage
- Willing to take risks
- A "rebel" attitude to compete against large incumbents
- Strong financial projection and modeling capabilities

Venture Capitalist Examples

- Megan is a junior analyst at a VC firm that invests in start-ups in the media industry. She maintains a set of Excel models that maintain rolling 12-month projections for each start-up's income statement, balance sheet, and cash flow statement. The primary reason to maintain these models is to track each start-up's "burn rate"— the pace at which a company spends its existing capital base. The models also project when a company may start generating revenue and when it may need to raise new capital.

- Sir Kensington's, a leading all-natural condiment company, announced the completion of an $8.5 million "Series A" equity-financing round. At the time, Sir Kensington's stated that it was the fastest-growing condiment brand in Whole Foods, where its ketchup, mayonnaise, and mustard products were Non-GMO Project Verified and made with simple, whole ingredients. Sir Kensington's mission was to compete against larger, more established condiment leaders such as Heinz ketchup, Kraft mayonnaise, and French's mustard, among many others.

  The financing was led by Verlinvest, a private-investment holding company focused on fast-growing branded consumer-product companies. In addition to its investment, Verlinvest acted as a long-term partner by helping management teams drive growth across channels and geographies, primarily in the food and beverage, retail/e-commerce, hospitality, and digital-marketing sectors. Verlinvest's previous investments included vitaminwater, Vita Coco, and popchips. The investment aimed to accelerate growth, expand product offerings, and make key hires.

  Sir Kensington's was acquired by global consumer products company Unilever less than two years after this VC funding. The price tag was reported at $140 million! Why would Unilever pay such a large price for a start-up company? Unilever already owns many consumer brands found in your grocery store such as Hellmans, Lipton, Ben & Jerry's, and Q-tips. Consider all the synergies achieved by adding Sir Kensington products into Unilever's existing global supply chain and distribution network.

- According to the *Wall Street Journal*, the investment arm of Google—known as Google Capital—led an estimated $850 million funding round for Airbnb that valued the home-rental company at $30 billion. The deal was designed in part to relieve some pressure for Airbnb to go public, so the company would have more funds to spend on overseas expansion. Airbnb was backed by two dozen investors including US venture-capital firms Sequoia Capital and Andreessen Horowitz and international groups China Broadband Capital and Temasek Holdings. The company also included at least six mutual-fund companies as investors, including Fidelity Investments, T. Rowe Price, and Morgan Stanley Investment Management.

Analyst #6

THIRD-PARTY MANAGEMENT
(Also known as External Management, Fund of Funds)

Career Path	Undergraduate Degree	Advanced Degree	Personality Type	Level of Teamwork
CIO	•Finance •Economics	•MBA •CFA •CAIA	Introvert	Medium

Overview

Third-party managers oversee investments for asset owners such as pension funds, sovereign-wealth funds, university endowments, insurance companies, and corporate treasurers. Third-party managers select outside asset managers—buy-side, hedge-fund, private-equity, and venture-capital firms—to invest the asset owner's money.

Third-party managers exist for two reasons. First, certain asset owners do not want to invest in the infrastructure required to build an entire asset management team. They want to avoid hiring analysts and investing in office space, computer systems, and trading software. Why invest in this infrastructure when hundreds of asset managers already have it?

The second reason is a scaled-down version of the first. Insurance companies or pension funds, for example, may have in-house fixed-income investment teams, economists, and traders. But they may wish to invest only 80% of their assets in fixed income. They require help investing the remainder in equities, private equity, venture capital, real estate, or other areas. Third-party management teams within the company oversee investments in these specialized areas outside their team's core competency.

Third-party managers will not make day-to-day specific buy-and-sell decisions. But they need to be aware of industry and macro trends, historical performance, and investments made by the third parties so they can design broad investment themes. Some investments may be in complex structured-finance securities such as collateralized loan obligations or mortgage-backed securities. A third-party manager defers many investment decisions to external asset managers but needs to understand the risk profiles and specifics of each investment.

Third-Party Manager: What will I do?

- Screen asset managers—interview asset managers and review their investment track record, career background, company liquidity, investment philosophies, and what's known as connections with "deal flow". This means the ability to take part in a popular investment such as an initial public offering or a promising start-up's new funding round
- Develop a strong understanding of the underlying investments
- Develop a strong understanding of alternative assets such as real estate, private equity, and structured finance securities
- Understand the legal structures and terms of an investment: what is the mandatory holding period ("lock-up" period)? What are the investor's voting rights? What is a fund's dividend policy? What are the capital calls and dilution requirements? What is the liquidation preference of an investment if the asset manager goes bankrupt?
- Assess asset manager fees including the fee known as "2 and 20" from hedge funds (a 2% flat fee plus 20% of any profits)
- Have a broad understanding of global economy and geopolitical landscapes
- Construct portfolios based on a firm's risk appetite and diversification needs
- Set investment guidelines such as limits on emerging markets or non-dividend-paying stocks

Third-Party Manager: What skills and qualities help?

- Enjoy broad macro topics related to different asset classes
- Enjoy portfolio construction and quantitative-related considerations, such as correlations and benchmarking performance
- Tolerant of having limited control over day-to-day decision making around security buying and selling. Third-party managers set initial guidelines for risk tolerance but buy-and-sell decisions are delegated to external asset managers

Third-Party Examples

- According to the *Wall Street Journal,* third-party managers at the state of New Jersey's pensions have committed about $1 billion to private-equity firm Blackstone's Tactical Opportunities fund, a catchall for deals that don't fit elsewhere. At the time of the article, the fund had invested $6.8 billion and bought or financed assets as diverse as ships, land beneath cell towers, and a Canadian diamond mine. The fund is also one of the largest providers of reverse mortgages.
- State University has an endowment of $20 billion. The endowment historically allocates 100% of its investments to investment-grade corporate bonds. It has a staff of 15 dedicated to that mandate. This includes a team of buy-side fixed-income analysts and a small trading desk. As interest rates fell, State's chief investment officer decided to optimize returns by shifting 10% of its portfolio into high-yield bank loans and another 10% into equities. The goal was to earn higher risk-adjusted returns. Since the high-yield bank loan and equity markets have nuances different from the investment grade corporate-bond market, State hired individuals for an external management team. This team would be responsible for meeting with dozens of asset managers to assess their capabilities, historical performance, investment philosophies, and fees. From this initial screening process, the

third-party team would ultimately select two asset managers to run the new portfolio.

- Kentucky's retirement system (KRS) oversees the pensions and insurance for thousands of police officers, prison guards, and city, county, and state workers. In total, KRS oversees more than $15 billion in total investments. Ten percent, or $1.5 billion, was historically allocated to hedge funds. KRS announced plans to withdraw $800 million of the $1.5 billion committed to hedge funds to limit investment fees and reduce its portfolio's complexity. The plan aimed to reduce the exposure from 10% to 8% over the first several months, and then further decrease to approximately 5% of total assets.

Analyst #7

RATINGS AGENCY ANALYST

Career Path	Undergraduate Degree	Advanced Degree	Personality Type	Level of Teamwork
•MD/Partner •CIO (indirect, via move to buy-side)	•Finance •Economics	•MBA •CFA •MS in Finance	Varies	Low

Overview

Rating agencies play an important role in debt markets. Their ratings serve as a stake in the ground for bond pricing. The agencies determine a borrower's ability to repay principal and interest to a lender. The ratings serve as a starting point for price setting although the market determines final values.

A rating-agency analyst is similar to the fixed-income buy-side and sell-side roles. They analyze a company's operations including its product, competition, and supply chain. The analyst also must be knowledgeable about capital structures, including security claims on assets, guarantees, subordination risk, and legal covenants. Unlike the buy-side, however, rating-agency analysts do not invest money. And unlike the sell-side, they do not offer opinions on relative value or pricing data. Instead, rating agencies play a more defined role of placing letter-grade ratings on a bond issuance.

Each agency has about 10 "investment grade" letter ratings, ranging from AAA/Aaa (highest) to BBB–/Baa3 (lowest). They also provide about a dozen "high-yield" ratings ranging from BB+/Ba1 (highest) to the single-C area, which represents near- or at-bankruptcy levels. Lower rated bonds are considered riskier for investors so they typically offer a higher yield to attract investors.

The rating-agency industry is dominated by three agencies: S&P, Moody's, and Fitch. In addition to rating bonds issued by public companies, the agencies rate bonds issued by cities and government agencies, known as public finance. They also cover the structured debt discussed at the beginning of the analyst chapter.

Ratings Agency Analyst: What will I do?

- Rate debt with different letter grades across different types of bonds, including corporate bonds, public bonds, sovereign debt, mortgage-backed securities, and asset-backed debt
- Determine the relative risk level of a borrower's ability to repay all principal and interest to a lender in a timely manner
- Monitor ratings on an ongoing basis
- Write research detailing company operations, competitive landscapes, capital structures, and legal covenants
- Examine bonds to provide a grade rather than to invest money
- Meet with investors and host events to discuss ratings and outlooks
- Model financial results and projections

Ratings Agency Analyst: What skills and qualities help?

- Analytically curious
- Enjoy reading financial statements
- Enjoy writing, including long research reports
- Like creating financial models, projections, and sensitivity scenarios
- Like to travel to meet with companies and buy-side investors
- Ability to handle market volatility
- Ability to tolerate public scrutiny as all ratings must be publicly disseminated to the markets in a detailed press release or report
- Eager to live in a global financial center such as New York, London, Chicago, or Singapore

Ratings Agency Analyst Examples

- Agilent Technologies manufactures instruments that analyze the physical and biological properties of substances and products. Their products include equipment to measure water or soil contaminants. The company issued $300 million senior unsecured notes due in 2026 that Moody's, S&P, and Fitch rated Baa1/BBB/BBB+ respectively. The rating agencies mentioned strong market share and conservative fiscal policies as their rationale for the relatively solid ratings. Market pricing showed that investors agreed with the rating agencies as the bonds sold just below par at $99.624 at a coupon of 3.050% for a yield of 3.094%. The pricing was in line with other similarly rated entities.

- S&P Global Ratings assigned an A+ long-term rating to the Illinois Finance Authority's $73 million series 2016 revenue refunding bonds. All bonds were issued for Riverside Health System (RHS). In its press release, S&P wrote: "We continue to assess RHS's financial profile as very strong and view the enterprise profile as strong. The very strong financial profile reflects RHS's robust financial performance and sound liquidity and financial flexibility. And the strong enterprise profile reflects our view of its stable market position and strategy and the limited economic fundamentals reflecting the size of the population of the primary service area."

- Fitch Ratings affirmed nine classes of bonds tied to various commercial mortgages in the 7 World Trade Center Office in New York. The classes of bonds had ratings ranging from BBB to AAA. The commercial mortgage-backed security (CMBS) certificates are scheduled to amortize fully by their maturity dates following an initial interest-only (IO) period.

  Fitch stated that the affirmation of the bonds was based on the stable performance of the underlying collateral. Property performance has remained stable, with solid tenancy and limited upcoming rollover. Occupancy was 94.8% and the net cash flow debt service coverage ratio was 1.24x.

Fitch stated that the four largest tenants occupy over 70% of the property, all with long-term leases containing renewal options. The largest tenants include Moody's Corporation (46% of total property square footage), Wilmer Hale LLP (12%), Royal Bank of Scotland (8%), and MSCI, Inc. (7%). Fitch further stated that that the building is considered a high quality Manhattan asset comprised of 52-stories totaling approximately 1.7 million square feet in close proximity to several modes of major transportation.

- The advertising industry is inherently volatile, as it is easy for companies to reduce advertising spending during economic downturns. During the 2008–2009 US recession, the advertising market was hit especially hard. TV conglomerate CBS Corporation (owner of the CBS Network, Showtime Television, CBS Radio, and other businesses) issued a press release in October 2008 stating that the economic slowdown had adversely affected advertising revenues and was likely to cause further advertising spending declines. The company revised its 2008 full-year business outlook, including a revision in earnings per share of $0.43 for the third quarter of 2008, compared to $0.51 for the third quarter of 2007. The company expected to incur a non-cash impairment charge of approximately $14 billion to reduce the carrying value of goodwill and intangible assets related to FCC licenses and investments.

The news was the start of a tumultuous period for the company. Its stock price dipped below $5 per share amid speculation the company might declare bankruptcy. Prior to the recession, CBS's debt was rated Baa3/BBB/BBB all with stable outlooks by Moody's, S&P, and Fitch, respectively. In the months after the initial announcement, S&P moved its ratings to BBB– with a negative outlook, putting the company on the brink of high-yield status. The bond markets already felt the company was in high-yield territory, with the yields on some of its debt trading in excess of 10%, signifying a material risk of default. The company announced a cut to its dividend to save cash. When the company reported its 2009 financial statements, results were as bad as expected as operating income plunged 60% from the 2007 pre-recession period.

Despite the market panic, Fitch maintained its BBB rating with a stable outlook throughout the entire recessionary period. Fitch cited a belief that the weakness was concentrated on the local advertising market and said the national advertising market for the CBS Network, as well as the syndication and Showtime businesses all remained strong.

The following two years saw a dramatic financial recovery for CBS, with 2011 operating income shooting back to 2007 levels (a 150% increase over 2009!). Bond spreads normalized back to investment-grade levels, and S&P and Moody's both moved their ratings up in line with Fitch at "Baa2 stable outlook" and "BBB stable outlook," respectively.

Analyst #8

COMMERCIAL BANKER: CREDIT OFFICER
(Also known as Loan Underwriter, Middle-Market Lender)

Career Path	Undergraduate Degree	Advanced Degree	Personality Type	Level of Teamwork
CIO	•Finance •Economics	•MBA •CFA •MS in Finance	Introvert	Medium

Overview

The commercial banker career falls into two areas: credit officer, which is discussed here, and relationship manager, which is covered in the "Bucket #3: Matchmakers" section. Even though they are separate careers, there is a close relationship between the two and also with the investment banker roles discussed later. Employers in the commercial banking space include traditional banks such as Bank of America, Wells Fargo, and Citibank.

A commercial banker credit officer is similar to the buy-side fixed-income analyst role. Both lend money to corporations or public institutions and both need to perform due-diligence analysis to determine the risk of not being paid back in full and the appropriate cost (interest rate) that risk merits. For example, a strong business like Microsoft would have a high probability of repaying a loan and therefore require a low interest rate. Conversely, a weak business profile such as a newspaper or radio broadcaster would require a much higher interest rate to compensate for the risk of default.

Beyond the similarities around credit analysis, the commercial banker and fixed-income buy-side roles differ slightly. Buy-side analysts lend money in the form of bonds while commercial bankers extend credit using bank revolvers and term loans. Additionally, buy-side analysts buy and sell bonds on a regular basis, whereas credit officers typically make an initial loan and are not actively involved in buying and selling on a secondary market.

Bank revolvers and term loans are typically completed in syndicate form. This means multiple banks spread the risk. The largest lenders and primary arrangers receive the largest fees. For example, a $1 billion bank revolver led by Bank of America could be comprised of 10 lenders. The syndication to the other nine banks is covered in the investment banking section later in this book.

It's worth noting that fees from investment banking can determine whether a bank lends to a company. A credit officer may feel 100% confident that a company will pay back its loans but if additional fees from treasury or investment banking services do not earn that bank a proper return on capital, the relationship manager could decline the loan. This fee generation from other business is discussed in the relationship manager and investment banking roles.

Middle-market lending is the term used for loans to smaller companies. These loans are sometimes done by specialized asset managers that are not tied to a traditional bank so the credit officer drives the lending decision making.

Commercial Banker: Credit Officer: What will I do?

- Provide opinion on whether bank loans should be approved (also known as underwriting)
- Manage a portfolio of bank revolvers and bank loans
- Analyze a company's ability to pay interest and principal on loans using financial statement and business analysis
- Conduct "SWOT" analysis: assess the strengths, weaknesses, opportunities and threats of a business you are considering for a loan
- Study a borrower to determine its prospects and detect potential "cliff risks" – the threats to a company's business model due to competitive or technological changes

- Model historical financial results and project future expectations and cash flows
- Develop expertise in specific industries
- For a specialized group, focus on real estate transactions such as construction loans

Commercial Banker: Credit Officer: What skills and qualities help?

- Like working with numbers
- Enjoy reading financial statements
- Enjoy investigating the outlook for companies and industries
- Not intimidated by taking very calculated risks
- A team player who is tolerant of having credit decisions over-ruled due to fee decisions or other relationship issues

Commercial Banker Credit Officer Examples

- Credit officers must be detail oriented and willing to create complex loans. Commercial bankers for JPMorgan Chase Bank, Bank of America, and Wells Fargo led a $1 billion unsecured multi-currency revolving credit facility syndicate for diversified global manufacturer Dover Corporation. The facility runs for five years. Borrowings on the facility can be in the form of various currencies such as the US dollar, Canadian dollar, Euros, Swedish kroners, or British pounds. Interest rates are based on local currency rates, plus an applicable margin ranging from 0.58% to 1%. Under this facility, Dover must maintain an interest-coverage ratio of earnings before interest, tax, and depreciation and amortization (EBITDA) to net-interest expense of not less than 3:1. This allows the lenders to feel comfortable that they will be repaid.
- Commercial bankers from Bank of America, Bank of Nova Scotia, Bank of Tokyo-Mitsubishi, HSBC Bank, and BNP Paribas, among others, led a $900 million asset-securitization loan facility

to Arrow Electronics, a global distributor of electronic and industrial components. The loan facility was collateralized by the accounts receivable of some of Arrow's subsidiaries. The interest rate is based on the company's credit ratings.

In both examples, the credit officers for the banks need a strong understanding of the borrowers' financial statements, business profile, strengths and weaknesses, and potential threats.

- Alex works for ABC Capital, a commercial lender that specializes in loans to "middle-market" entities – companies with revenues of $100 million or less. Due to his client's relatively small size, Alex requires much deeper due diligence than a commercial banker would require when lending to a Fortune 500 global company that has investment grade ratings and billions of dollars in revenues. This due diligence includes on-site visits, monthly financial statements, and quarterly compliance calculations. The small size also requires ABC Capital to make sure it has first-lien security on all assets, such as real estate, accounts receivables, inventory, and intellectual property, in exchange for the loans.
- Lawrence is a credit officer for XYZ Bank. He has approval to lend to high-risk corporations through the bank's leveraged-loan portfolio. These loans are made on a first-lien-secured basis, meaning that if the borrower goes into bankruptcy, XYZ will have first claim on all assets until it fully recovers its loan value. One reason the company allows Lawrence to make risky loans is that the company does not intend to hold the loans itself. Instead, XYZ sells its loans to ABC Management. ABC specializes in a structured-debt instrument known as a CLO (Collateralized Loan Obligation). These CLOs pool dozens of bank loans that are diversified by industry and geography. ABC sells these CLOs to hedge funds and asset managers seeking higher-yielding investments with the diversification and security that CLOs offer compared to traditional high-yield bonds.
- Chris received a joint MBA-JD (law) degree during his graduate-school work. He is also a Chartered Financial Analyst (CFA).

Upon graduation from graduate school, Chris was hired by a major commercial bank to work in their "work-out" group, a division that specializes in the bankruptcy process for defaulted loans made by a bank's credit division. These are loans made by commercial bankers that ultimately default on interest or principal payments or both. The law degree gives Chris the ability to determine legal claims on assets, guarantees from subsidiaries, intellectual property rights, and overall liquidation recovery through a bankruptcy court. The MBA and CFA charter help Chris with valuations for the business outlook of the defaulted company.

- Commercial bankers are active in construction and commercial loans for large real estate projects. An area on the west side of New York City known as Hudson Yards has experienced a construction boom over the past several years. A new subway line extension benefited the area and helped make it a tourist attraction. The *Wall Street Journal* estimated that a seven-building construction project in the area was financed with $18 billion in equity and debt capital, the latter provided by commercial banks such as Bank of America, Wells Fargo, Deutsche Bank, and HSBC Holdings. A credit officer likely recognized the area's strong potential.

- Many large industrial companies such as Caterpillar, Deere, Ford, and IBM have a "captive finance" subsidiary that originates loans for their customers. These subsidiaries provide customers loans to buy the vehicles, bulldozers, or computer systems. Though not technically employed by a bank, people filling these jobs and other types of asset-based lending are part of the credit officer commercial banker career.

Analyst #9

WEALTH MANAGEMENT
(Also known as Private Banking, Financial Advisor, Investment Advisor, Financial Planner, Family Office, Private Client)

Career Path	Undergraduate Degree	Advanced Degree	Personality Type	Level of Teamwork
MD/Partner	•Finance •Economics	•MBA •CFA •JD •LLM in Tax	Extrovert	Low

Overview

Although wealth management professionals must be well-versed in economics and finance, the role relies more on managing relationships and accommodating client goals than the deep-dive financial analysis required for buy-side, sell-side, and hedge-fund analysts. Typical clients are wealthy individuals and families with brokerage accounts at places such as JPMorgan Chase, Citibank, Morgan Stanley, and Charles Schwab. A wealth manager is the point of contact for those clients.

A wealth management professional must understand a client's risk tolerance and work with portfolio managers to build a suitable portfolio of investments including stocks, bonds, and mutual funds. The wealth manager's main role is to assist clients in building, managing, protecting, and transitioning wealth. This includes investments and banking services and providing insurance products. In addition, a wealth manager needs to relay important information to clients: What is the "house view" on the economy? Why is the company recommending selling or buying specific investments? What are a transaction's tax implications?

Beyond portfolio construction and management, some wealth managers offer "family office services" such as trust and estate planning, bill paying, bookkeeping, tax expertise, and other concierge services, typically for high-net-worth individuals. This book does not have a specific section on personal accountants and tax advisors. These individuals can be employed by a wealth manager and often have an accounting degree and CPA designation.

Wealth Management: What will I do?

- Serve as the point person for individual clients
- Provide clients a broad understanding of the global economy and geopolitical landscapes
- Provide personal finance expertise with a command of investment vehicles
- Explain the tax implications of products such as traditional IRAs, Roth IRAs, and tax-sheltered annuities
- Understand fundamental and relative analysis of investments including price-earnings ratios, price-earnings growth ratios, and dividend yield, among many others
- Understand clients' age-appropriate risk appetite and how asset allocations accomplish investment and retirement goals
- Prospect for new clients
- Perform individual financial planning and budgeting including income needs
- Develop a broad understanding of all services—investments, individual and estate-tax planning, insurance, and bookkeeping.

Wealth Management: What skills and qualities help?

- Enjoy advising individual clients and comfortable making investment recommendations
- Ability to handle market volatility
- Tolerant of clients with very demanding personalities
- Comfortable delivering unfavorable news when investments underperform
- Outgoing personality with an ability to discuss markets, securities, economics, travel, politics, sports, and other topics a client may enjoy

- Enjoy travel
- Sales and networking skills to build client list

Wealth Management Examples

- Kenny is a wealth manager at ABC Securities. He manages a total portfolio of $500 million for 60 individuals with an average net worth of $8.3 million each. His clients are located throughout the Northwest and he travels regularly to meet with them and to take them to dinners, shows, and sporting events. He generated his first dozen clients by cold-calling in a position after graduating from college. His other clients were referred by his initial clients. Kenny works closely with a team that constructs optimal portfolios based on historical correlations and back-testing of mutual fund and stock combinations. The portfolios are composed of mutual funds that offer broad diversification across developed and emerging markets.
- Steven is a wealth manager at ABC Bank. The bank has major branches on five different continents that allow it to provide attentive customer service to high-net-worth individuals who travel and have multiple properties around the world. Given the bank's global scale, Steven accepts only clients with a net worth exceeding $25 million. Steven attends weekly meetings with the bank's economist and strategist team to hear their views on the economy and markets.
- Lawrence is a financial advisor for XYZ Securities. He has dozens of clients. One of his clients is a 30-year-old professional who received a $1 million inheritance. Lawrence has advised this client to invest the $1 million in small-cap and technology mutual funds. Lawrence believes the clients' young age gives her time to ride out stock market volatility and that the high-growth profile of these mutual funds will generate the highest returns over a long-term investment horizon. Additionally, the client's current job provides enough monthly income to forgo the need for dividend-paying stocks or interest income from bonds.

- Another of Lawrence's clients is 65 and recently retired from his job with a lump-sum $1 million pension. Lawrence has advised this client to invest half of the $1 million in a portfolio of large-cap dividend-paying stocks and the other half in a portfolio of corporate and public bonds. Lawrence's rationale is that the client will no longer have a salary to draw on for monthly expenses. The after-tax dividend and interest income from these portfolios will be more than enough to offset the client's living expenses. At the same time, Lawrence likes the low-volatility of large-cap stocks and corporate bonds.

- Young works for a local family office. The office caters to individuals with a net worth of $5 million or more. Services include bill paying, wealth management and advisory, and estate and tax planning. The family office has an exclusive deal with ABC Securities to execute all trades and to assist with portfolio construction. Young meets with clients to determine their risk tolerance and works with ABC to construct a suitable portfolio of stocks and bonds.

Analyst #10

CONSULTANT

Career Path	Undergraduate Degree	Advanced Degree	Personality Type	Level of Teamwork
MD/Partner	•Strategy •Various other	MBA	Varies	Varies

Overview

The consultant career is challenging to define because the spectrum of duties is so broad. It does not fit neatly in this book's three-bucket structure but belongs best in the analyst category.

Consultants can touch every career discussed in this book including product management, business development, sales, strategy, accounting, tax, operations, marketing, human resources, investor relations, and asset management. Additionally, consultants can have varied expertise, from very high-level industry knowledge to very narrow and specific operational knowledge. The focus can vary from improving specific processes, to cutting costs, to implementing a new strategic vision. This section generally focuses on what is known as "management consulting".

Many classes in business school, especially MBA school, focus on "case studies." Case studies detail a specific background and situation a company faces. The situations can range from a crisis that needs an immediate fix, such as a competitor launching a new superior product, to more gradual improvements, such as increasing customer loyalty at a retailer or improving an inefficient work flow. Professors assemble students into teams with the task of finding the most optimal way to address a situation. Student teams assess the situation, devise a plan, and present it to the professor and class. Think of the consulting career as a lifetime of case studies, except your audience is composed of company executives instead of professors.

The biggest value consultants add is often prior experience. Consider someone who spent 30 years in supply-chain management for an industrial company. This person would likely make a strong consultant in their area of expertise. Beyond experience, consultants add value by offering fresh and unbiased perspectives to management teams that may be too complacent with legacy operations (often known as "change management"). Consultants also add value in their position as aggregators— they view and assess the actions of many different management teams across many different companies. This allows them to determine the best practices for their client base.

Management Consultant: What will I do?

- Provide a fresh, unbiased view of a company's strategic and competitive position and make recommendations to improve
- Provide a fresh, unbiased view on a company's operational processes, cost structure, and management layers and recommend how to improve. This can include expertise around reducing costs and restructuring operations
- Advise clients on industry best practices
- Understand new customer trends and preferences and how those may impact an industry or company
- Perform "SWOT" analysis: what are the strengths, weaknesses, opportunities and threats of a situation on which you are consulting

Management Consultant: What skills and qualities help?

- Fresh, innovative thinker
- Problem solver
- Enjoy strategic thinking around how to improve a product, service, or process
- Comfortable with public speaking and presenting to senior executives

- Prefer variety of advising many clients rather than working at a single company
- Ability to handle extensive travel
- Knowledge of technology and automation
- Comfortable in a career that is largely an outsider role—you are never a member of the company or team you advise

Management Consultant Examples

- Leading consulting firm The Boston Consulting Group publishes short-form "insights" on important issues companies may face. The insights detail strategies such as how clients can deal with a large supplier that has significant leverage, how to optimize an advertising and marketing budget through better planning, fee negotiation, and how to improve the product-design process. The material gives potential clients tangible recommendations and serves as marketing material to alert customers about the consulting the company provides.
- Leading consulting firm Bain & Company consulted for a local TV broadcaster client ("BroadcastCo"). The client's CEO was interested in a complete redesign of the company's sales and digital strategy. In pursuit of these objectives, BroadcastCo asked Bain to develop a digital sales strategy that aligned with current market trends. BroadcastCo's digital audience was growing but their sales were lagging.

  Bain stated that their approach to developing BroadcastCo's digital sales strategy sought to answer four key questions:

  1) What is the size of the digital market and who should BroadcastCo target?
  2) How should BroadcastCo "go to market" in pursuit of these targets?
  3) How should BroadcastCo organize their digital team for success?
  4) What is the opportunity for BroadcastCo?

In order to answer these questions, Bain conducted a survey of more than 1,500 local advertisers to determine their media preferences, purchasing patterns, and decision making criteria to determine the segments to target. Bain also analyzed BroadcastCo's current operations (digital inventory, audience growth, and sell-out rates) and management's internal structure (sales strategy, management layers).

Based on its analysis, Bain made recommendations to make BroadcastCo's sales team more knowledgeable about customer needs and to have a better understanding of its digital capabilities. This ultimately led to a more streamlined management structure including new roles for business development and new centralized support functions. Bain stated that after the organizational refresh, BroadcastCo committed to a 40% revenue increase in their digital business, outpacing the market.

- Leading consulting firm Accenture helped its client Mondelēz International establish significant savings. Mondelēz is a global snack food company that owns popular brands OREO®, NABISCO® and CADBURY®. Although Mondelēz experienced high growth, it needed to improve operating margins, which were lower than its peers due to high expenses. Mondelēz asked Accenture to establish a zero-based budgeting system to help it compete in an increasingly challenging economic environment. A zero-based budget is a bottoms-up annual process that "cleans the slate" each year—just because a team spent $10 million last year does not mean that team automatically starts with a $10 million budget the following year. Instead, management needs to justify each dollar in the new year.

While Mondelēz sought to streamline operations, it also wanted to preserve key attributes that made it a successful company. Accenture focused on taking costs out of low-value areas such as travel and other overhead so Mondelēz could reinvest the money in areas creating a competitive advantage, such as product development and marketing.

In just three months, Mondelēz's new operating model was up and running. In the first year, the company delivered savings of $350 million. Over three years, the company aimed to save $1 billion. The savings helped increase operating margins. In addition, Accenture stated that the new budgeting processes and change management program helped embed cost consciousness in day-to-day operations and culture.

- Sue is an operations consultant. Her expertise is in helping retailers design store flow to make the customer experience as seamless as possible. Sue believes a retail best practice is to move towards open floor plans while eliminating lines at a central cashier. Sue advises her clients to achieve this by installing self-checkout kiosks, as well as by arming store employees with hand held credit card readers so customers can pay without waiting in a checkout line.

Bucket #3: Matchmakers

A s the name suggests, a matchmaker career revolves around introducing buyers, sellers, managers, and asset owners to each other. Compensation in these careers usually relies heavily on bonuses tied to the volume of deals completed. We discussed the careers "Sell-side Analyst" and "Sell-side Economist/Strategist" in the previous section but be aware that some careers in this Bucket #3—investment banking, trading, and institutional sales—can also be referred to as "sell-side" roles. Additionally, those five careers are probably the most typical "Wall Street" jobs in this book. The term "working on Wall Street" gets thrown around and can refer to the buy-side, hedge fund, private equity, and rating agency jobs previously discussed. But the purest Wall Street job designations belong to the sell-side analyst, sell-side economist/strategist, investment banker (especially capital markets advisory), sell-side trader, and institutional sales careers.

Careers in the matchmaker section can be considered in three ways:

1.) **Industry Focus**: Similar to the practitioner and analyst sections, the commercial banking relationship manager typically covers a specific industry. For example, a commercial banker may cover only the pharmaceutical industry or the food and beverage industry.

2.) **Specialty Focus**: Investment banking is typically grouped into specialty areas such as mergers & acquisitions, debt capital markets and equity capital markets. These are discussed in more detail in the following pages.

3.) **Product Focus**: Unlike any other career discussed in this book, careers in trading and institutional sales can focus on specific financial products such as options, foreign exchange forwards, commodity futures, and interest rate swaps.

Most matchmaker careers typically are established directly out of college after a candidate earns an undergraduate or MBA degree. It is challenging to move into this path years into a different career so try to decide early if it is for you.

This book excludes various broker and agent careers such as real-estate broker, staffing and executive search since they are more specialized than careers someone typically pursues when studying general business. But those types of careers fall into this match-making bucket.

Matchmaker #1

COMMERCIAL BANKER: RELATIONSHIP MANAGER

Career Path	Undergraduate Degree	Advanced Degree	Personality Type	Level of Teamwork
MD/Partner	•Finance •Economics	MBA	Extrovert	High

Overview

A commercial banker relationship manager is the primary banking contact for a corporation's chief financial officer and treasurer. The relationship manager works with the credit officer to provide bank loans to a borrower, and with investment bankers for capital market and merger and acquisition transactions. The relationship manager is also the point person for treasury services, such as bank account set-up and investment products for excess cash.

Most banks lend to clients as an entrée to higher-fee businesses, such as the work performed by investment banks. A bank that does not extend credit to a borrower can be at a disadvantage when approaching a chief financial officer about other business, such as merger and acquisition advisory.

Commercial Banker Relationship Manager: What will I do?

- Develop and manage client relationships
- Serve as the point person to connect chief financial officers and treasurers of client companies with the investment-banking side (this role is often viewed as part of investment-banking)
- Function as a strategic advisor to clients around asset-liability management, deal financing and various treasury services
- Work with credit officers to lend money to companies

- Ensure profitable relationships, factoring in total fees from cash management, interest income, and advisory fees in exchange for lending money
- Maintain expertise of a client's business model and industry

Commercial Banker Relationship Manager: What skills and qualities help?

- Problem solver and strategic thinker; consistently finding creative ideas to benefit your employer and your client
- Enjoy interfacing with clients including entertaining
- Good awareness of current events with a broad understanding of macro environment

Commercial Banker Relationship Manager Examples

- Mary is a commercial banker for ABC Bank and serves as the relationship manager for her client XYZ Company. XYZ has $500 million in debt that is all fixed-rate bonds. XYZ also exports over 50% of its products to Europe, resulting in significant currency exposure to the British pound and euro. XYZ operates in a very fragmented industry that Mary believes is overdue for consolidation. Every three months, Mary takes the XYZ chief financial officer to lunch with different members of ABC's investment-banking team. On one occasion, she included an investment banker who handles fixed-to-floating interest rate swaps to explain that they expect interest rates to decline which would allow XYZ to save money by swapping some fixed-rate debt for floating rates using derivative instruments. This month she will introduce ABC's currency expert who will explain currency forwards and "collars" to hedge XYZ's pound and euro exposure. Eventually Mary will connect ABC's head of mergers and acquisitions with XYZ's chief financial officer to discuss potential acquisition targets and valuations.
- Morgan Stanley led a deal that extended a $1.15 billion 5% bank loan to private start-up ride-hailing company Uber Technologies,

according to *The Wall Street Journal.* The loan helped alleviate the need to raise additional equity, avoiding dilution of existing private shareholders. Barclays, Citigroup, and Goldman Sachs also participated in the deal. The deal was unusual because banks typically do not extend credit to start-up companies.

Given Uber's start-up status and media reports at the time of this publication that the company was losing money, one could conclude that the decision to make this loan was driven by a relationship manager and the investment banking side of the business rather than by the credit officer discussed earlier. The loan is likely an entrée into Uber for these banks to vie to take the company public in an initial public offering in the future. The banks would also hope to gain other types of investment and commercial banking fee business.

Matchmaker #2

INVESTMENT BANKER: MERGER AND ACQUISITION ADVISORY

Career Path	Undergraduate Degree	Advanced Degree	Personality Type	Level of Teamwork
MD/Partner	•Finance •Strategy •Economics	•MBA •MBA-JD	Extrovert	Medium

Overview

The investment banker in mergers and acquisition (M&A) advisory identifies potential acquisition targets and buyers of assets for clients. This person collaborates with the relationship commercial banker to determine a client's growth plans and appropriate businesses or assets to buy. These individuals will typically work with the chief executive officer (CEO), chief financial officer (CFO), treasurer, and strategy and corporate-development executives of a client. Those company executives may also have businesses or assets that no longer fit their strategic profile so they rely on an M&A investment banker to locate potential buyers.

Beyond the initial brainstorming and screening phases, an M&A banker is responsible for advising clients on valuations and overall deal structures given the banker's experience with similar deals. These terms and comparisons ("comps") are ultimately presented to a board of directors for approval.

Investment Banker M&A Advisory: What will I do?

- Advise companies on M&A targets using strategies that identify new growth paths or additional value through cost synergies
- Advise companies on optimal deal structures and tax considerations

- Advise companies on potential buyers for their noncore assets using a thorough understanding of market prices, valuations for assets and tax issues
- Conduct due diligence to determine deal pricing and terms and conditions
- Present recommendations to executive management and board of directors
- Work with legal advisors on terms and conditions

Investment Banker M&A Advisory: What skills and qualities help?

- Solid academic record from a respected college
- Strong financial analysis skills, including the ability to value businesses and assets using discounted cash flows and market multiple analysis
- Enjoy deal making
- Willing to travel significantly
- Willing to work very long hours
- Analytically curious
- Some level of sales mentality—need to pitch deals to potential clients
- Accept very little subjectivity with performance reviews which are largely based on the volume of deals closed

Investment Banker M&A Advisory Examples

- Banking and payment-technology company Fidelity National Information Services (FIS) agreed to acquire SunGard, a software-application company that specialized in the asset- and wealth-management industries. FIS would acquire 100% of the equity of SunGard. FIS would issue a combination of cash and stock valuing the company at $9.1 billion, including the assumption of SunGard debt. The combined company would have more than $9.2 billion in annual revenues. Bank of America Merrill

Lynch and Centerview Partners acted as financial advisors to FIS. Willkie Farr & Gallagher served as FIS's legal advisors in the transaction. Goldman Sachs & Co., JPMorgan Chase, Barclays, Deutsche Bank Securities, and Credit Suisse acted as financial advisors to SunGard. Simpson Thacher & Bartlett and Shearman & Sterling served as SunGard's legal advisors.

All the different parties involved are mentioned because the $9.1 billion valuation in the above example requires material amounts of due diligence. That is, the investment bankers on both sides of the transaction had to use various methods to value the business being acquired. Anyone entering the M&A advisory field should be aware that a thorough understanding of financial analysis is required. Agreements are not struck based on a few executives chatting around a table. Shareholders demand substantial evidence to support an agreement.

The following timeline and analysis of an acquisition illustrates the point further and provides some flavor about the work merger and acquisition advisory professionals perform:

- Intel Corp. agreed to acquire Altera Corporation for $54 per share in an all-cash transaction valued at $16.7 billion. Altera's board of directors unanimously recommended that shareholders approve the offer. Altera's proxy statement, which is a request for a shareholder's vote, was filed with the Security and Exchange Commission and included a fairness opinion from Goldman Sachs & Co.

    The deal's timeline started about six months prior to the official announcement, as Intel and Altera initially met to discuss a licensing agreement for semiconductor technology. The licensing discussions morphed into preliminary merger discussions. Altera engaged Goldman Sachs & Co. as its financial advisor early in the process. Over that six-month period, Goldman Sachs met with or corresponded with Altera's management team more than 45 times to discuss valuations and proposal terms from Intel as well as options for Altera's management team to consider other interested buyers.

Goldman Sachs's fairness opinion in the proxy statement was more than seven pages long and included various valuation analyses such as:

- <u>Premia Analysis</u>: Premia analysis includes reviewing the average premium paid above a stock price for all technology-related M&A deals over the most recent six-year period. Goldman Sachs calculated a median premium of 35% to a target's stock price for the sample analysis. In other words, if an acquired company's stock was trading at $100 prior to a deal, the median acquisition price was $135 per share. Acquirers offer a premium to a target's stock price to incentivize a sale. Goldman Sachs calculated that Intel's $54-per-share offer represented a 55% premium to Altera's "undisturbed" stock price of $35 (the day prior to public speculation about a deal surfaced). Taking into account the analysis, Goldman Sachs applied a reference range of premia of 25–50% to the unaffected closing price of $35, implying a range of values per share of $43–$52. *In other words, the $54/share Intel offer exceeded the highest value of the range generated from the Premia Analysis.*

- <u>Selected Company Multiple Analysis</u>: Goldman Sachs included a second analysis reviewing existing trading multiples of similar technology companies. The investment bank listed the 10 most similar companies to Altera and reviewed how its stock price traded in relation to its revenue, earnings before interest, tax, depreciation and amortization (EBITDA), and net income on a current and projected basis. Goldman estimated the median enterprise value / EBITDA multiple for the 10 comparative companies was approximately 12x. The $54 Intel offer represented a multiple of 19x based on Altera's projections. The price-per-earnings (P/E) multiple had a similar premium assigned to it (29x from Intel versus a median of 20x for the other companies). *The second valuation analysis produced similar results—the Intel offer was higher than comparable market valuations.*

- <u>Selected Transaction Analysis</u>: Goldman also analyzed 15 M&A transactions in the technology sector that occurred in the four years prior to Intel's offer and examined how those deals fared with stock premiums and P/E multiples. The company calculated that a recent deal where semiconductor company Avago Technologies acquired Broadcom Corp. at an approximate 24% premium to its recently traded stock price and a 20x P/E ratio. While that deal reflected positively on Intel's $54 stock-price offer, the overall median for the 15 deals was more in line with Intel's offer with a stock-price premium of 41% and P/E of 30x. Taking into account the results of this analysis, Goldman Sachs determined a range of values per share of common stock of $30–$53. *Again, the $54/share offer from Intel exceeded even the high end of the Selected Transaction Analysis.*

- <u>DCF Analysis</u>: The final analysis Goldman Sachs prepared for Altera management was a discounted cash flow (DCF) analysis. A DCF analysis involves estimating future cash flows, terminal values of a company and discounting those values at a cost of capital to arrive at a final sum value. Think of it like receiving guaranteed payments in the future and consider that inflation will reduce that value over time. For example, $100 10 years from now is worth less than $100 today. Using a range of values, Goldman Sachs determined a range of illustrative present values per share of common stock of $43–$60. *The $54/share offer from Intel is slightly higher than the mid-point generated from the DCF Analysis.*

Using the relative values from different valuation techniques, Goldman Sachs made a convincing case that the $54-per-share price was fair to Altera stockholders. For its work, Goldman Sachs earned a $35 million transaction fee.

- Kevin is an investment banker for ABC Bank, a global institution that lends money and advises companies. Kevin specializes in M&A advisory for the pharmaceutical sector. He regularly attends meetings with his commercial-banking colleague Jeff. They meet with clients that have lines of credit and bank loans from ABC. Kevin briefs the client's chief financial officers on recent M&A trends in the pharmaceutical industry and presents a slide deck detailing potential acquisition or divestiture targets.

Kevin recently met with the chief financial officer and treasurer of Generic Pharmaceutical. He presented a slide deck detailing the synergies Generic Pharmaceutical could achieve by acquiring fellow pharmaceutical company XYZ Pharma. His rationale centered on their similar locations, underutilization of the companies' manufacturing sites, and overlap of employees dedicated to distribution and overhead such as legal, accounting, and finance. Kevin illustrated how Generic could eliminate 50% of XYZ's costs without impacting overall sales, thereby earning a return on investment on an acquisition in excess of the company's 10% cost of capital.

Matchmaker #2a

INVESTMENT BANKER: CAPITAL MARKETS

Career Path	Undergraduate Degree	Advanced Degree	Personality Type	Level of Teamwork
MD/Partner	•Finance •Strategy •Economics	•MBA •CFA	Extrovert	Medium

Overview

The capital markets investment banker collaborates with the relationship commercial banker to advise chief financial officers (CFO) and treasurers on the capital markets. This individual functions as the bridge between a company's CFO and treasurer and the equity and fixed-income buy-side and hedge-fund analysts. This person functions as an introducing agent, matching someone needing capital with someone who has capital to invest.

The investment banker capital-markets role is divided into equity and fixed-income categories. The equity side focuses on initial public offerings and additional common stock and preferred stock offerings. The fixed-income role focuses on bond instruments.

This job revolves around valuation analysis: how should a company's equity or debt be priced and why? The answer typically results from a combination of comparative analysis (the price of other companies), future projections, and, importantly, face-to-face discussions with buy-side and hedge-fund investors.

The investment banker capital-markets role is responsible for organizing what is referred to as "road shows." These are national and sometimes global tours for management to explain its company and strategy to investors. An investment banker will have follow-up conversations with investors to explore their potential demand for an offering and to discuss pricing. The more investor demand generated during road shows, the stronger pricing a company receives for its equity or debt offerings.

Investment Banker Capital Markets: What will I do?

- Advise company officials, such as chief executive officers, chief financial officers, and treasurers, about equity and debt capital markets
- Organize road shows and create "pitch books" to generate investor interest
- Establish pricing, timing, number of shares (equity), maturity schedules (debt), and covenants (debt)
- Assist company with SEC registration and other regulatory requirements
- Advise companies on private and alternative methods to raise capital if public equity or debt markets are not a realistic option
- If part of a larger bank, collaborate with a commercial banker on a total financing package, such as bank loans in addition to a public-bond offering
- Serve as the "arranger" of multiple banks in a bank-loan syndicate
- Underwrite equity and bond deals while taking the first position of risk with an expectation to syndicate the deal to other investors

Investment Banker Capital Markets: What skills and qualities help?

- Strong academic record from a reputable school
- Willingness to travel
- Willingness to work very long hours
- Enjoy deal making
- Some level of a sales mentality to pitch deals to clients
- Strong understanding of business strategies, industries, and financial markets

- An extroverted personality to advise clients and meet with investors
- Accept very little subjectivity with performance reviews which are largely based on the volume of deals

Investment Banker Capital Markets Examples

- Morgan Stanley, JPMorgan Chase, and Goldman Sachs advised Facebook on its May 2012 initial public offering. According to SEC filings, the company initially expected to price its offering at a range of $28–$35 per share. A few days before the actual IPO, the price range was increased to $34–$38 per share. On the day of the IPO, the company priced its stock at the high end of the range—$38 per share. The price increases in the days and weeks leading to the offering likely resulted from investor feedback during the road-show phase. This gave the company and its investment bankers confidence about investor demand.
- Meredith works in investment banking for ABC Bank. Her client, Generic Pharmaceuticals, considered seeking $1 billion from the bond markets to finance an acquisition. Generic requested that ABC arrange a set of meetings and conference calls with buy-side and hedge-fund fixed-income investors. Meredith worked with her institutional sales colleague to invite fixed-income investors to participate in two days of telephone meetings with Generic's chief financial officer and treasurer to discuss company operations, strategy, competitive landscape, and the terms of a bond offering. Each day included six time slots lasting 45 minutes with five to 10 investors. Meredith moderated each call, providing a brief introduction of the deal terms. She also facilitated a question and answer session. After the calls, Meredith and her team circled back with investors to determine their interest. Following her follow-up calls, Meredith advised Generic that it could raise the $1 billion in funds by structuring the deal as $500 million of 3.5% five-year notes and $500 million of 4.5% 10-year notes.

- When industrial conglomerates Johnson Controls (JC) and Tyco International merged, Bank of America Merrill Lynch, and Citigroup Global Markets advised the companies about a debt exchange and consent solicitation. JC and Tyco had $4.3 billion and $2.2 billion, respectively, of senior unsecured bonds at the time of the merger. The combined companies wanted to move all bonds from the individual entities to the new parent entity, Johnson Controls International. To incentivize bondholders to move their claims to the new parent, the company announced an offer to exchange the existing bonds for new bonds that had identical terms and conditions, plus bondholders would receive a $1 cash payment for every $1,000 worth of bonds owned if they promptly accepted. The offer had a consent solicitation which would result in any bonds not participating in the exchange losing certain covenants in the legal documents. These terms served as a carrot ($1 cash payment) and stick (removal of important covenants).

- After its exchange offer closed, Johnson Controls International went to the European bond markets and issued €1 billion of senior unsecured bonds via an underwriting agreement with a syndicate of investment banks. These banks did not intend to hold these bonds so promptly syndicated the bonds to buy-side and hedge fund clients, collecting fees along the way.

Matchmaker #2b

INVESTMENT BANKER: STRUCTURED FINANCE

Career Path	Undergraduate Degree	Advanced Degree	Personality Type	Level of Teamwork
MD/Partner	•Finance •Economics •Math/Statistics	•MBA •CFA •MBA-JD	Varies	Medium

Overview

A structured-finance investment banker essentially connects parties seeking an immediate payment with another party seeking steady series of payments over many years. To make that happen, these professionals create fixed-income securities backed by pools of financial assets. These could include mortgages, auto loans, credit card loans, and commercial real estate mortgages. These securities have names like commercial mortgage-backed securities (CMBS), residential mortgage-backed securities (RMBS), and asset-backed securities (ABS). Almost anything with a steady recurring cash flow can be securitized. In fact, bonds have been created that are backed by whole businesses like Dunkin' Donuts franchise agreements or a stream of royalty payments from a portfolio of music or movies.

An investment banker's role is to match owners of assets, such as banks, real estate owners, mortgage and loan originators, financial institutions, and government agencies with people interested in receiving the stream of money those assets generate, such as fixed-income buy-side and hedge-fund investors. An asset owner receives an immediate lump sum payment. In return, investors collect interest and principal from the pool of assets.

The main difference between structured-finance securities and traditional fixed-income securities is the "pooling" effect. All these securities are comprised of a pool of loans. A $1 billion CMBS, for example, could be comprised of 30 commercial mortgages spread across 30 states. What's more, the $1 billion can be split in different payment and bankruptcy priorities with the higher priority tiers receiving higher ratings from the rating agencies (and thus lower yields since they are perceived to be less risky). For an investor, pooling offers geographic diversification that reduces risk.

Structured finance securities are accompanied by large volumes of legal documents that specifically lay out how cash flows and assets are prioritized.

A structured-finance investment banker is responsible for aggregating these pools of loans, legally securitizing them into a single claim for investors, and marketing the final product to investors.

Employers in this field include all the large investment banks including Deutsche Bank, Bank of America, Citibank, Wells Fargo, Goldman Sachs, and Morgan Stanley.

Investment Banker Structured Finance: What will I do?

- Advise lenders and asset owners about monetizing their assets by pooling loans and selling them to investors
- Structure the securities backed by asset pool
- Create models to simulate potential cash flow outcomes and use model runs to determine bond sizing and amortization schedules.
- Work with lawyers to create legal and offering documents
- Explain deal to institutional sales colleagues as well as to potential investors via conference calls and roadshows
- Provide data, cash flow, and amortization modeling runs, legal documents, and other information to rating agencies to determine bond ratings

Investment Banker Structured Finance: What skills and qualities help?

- Often more quantitative and legal abilities than other investment-banking roles
- Strong modeling skills
- Willingness to work very long hours
- Comfortable advising clients and meeting with investors although an extroverted personality is less necessary than in a traditional investment-banker role.
- Accept very little subjectivity around performance reviews which are based on the volume of deals and fee income
- Willingness to travel

Investment Banker Structured Finance Examples

- Jacqueline is an investment banker for ABC Bank. She structures CMBS and coordinates with her institutional sales colleagues to sell the securities to buy-side investors. She recently structured a deal comprised of 10 classes of bonds rated AAA to BB. The collateral for the transaction is a pool of 52 commercial loans for office, retail, hotel, and multi-family properties located in Charlotte, Atlanta, Miami, Seattle, Portland, and San Francisco. Jacqueline spent two months meeting with the real-estate owners, doing site-visits, and working with a third-party law firm to draft the product's legal documents.

    When marketing the securities to investors, Jacqueline touts the geographic and building-type diversification, as well as the strong business fundamentals of the office tenants. Their businesses include financial services, pharmaceuticals, and media, all of which have a bullish outlook according to ABC Bank's sell-side analysts. Jacqueline and her colleagues have structured the CMBS to have an attractive 2x debt service coverage ratio. This means the rental income's cash flows are two times the amount needed to pay interest and principal-amortization payments, making the investment relatively safe.

- David is a public finance investment banker for a global bank. He works with commercial banking colleagues who specialize in loans to municipalities for large infrastructure projects. His colleagues are considering a $500 million "bridge loan" to a local county to improve their highway system. The bank is willing to make the $500 million construction loan with the goal of being paid back upon completion of the new highway. This will happen using a public revenue bond deal David will structure. The county plans to have a toll booth on the new highway. David and his team will structure a 30-year $500 million bond deal secured by future toll booth receipts. David plans to get this deal rated by the rating agencies. He will then market it to buy-side and hedge fund investors.

- Ronald is an investment banker for ABC Capital. He is responsible for structuring collateralized loan obligations (CLOs). These securities are pools of non-investment grade loans. By placing these loans into a CLO, the bank making the loans shares some of the risk with other investors. A CLO investor gets a one-stop shop for a pool of loans that provides greater diversification than buying loans outright. The typical deal is comprised of 100 or more underlying loans.

  Ronald recently completed structuring a five-year partially amortizing CLO paying 4.5% interest to investors. The CLO is comprised of 120 bank loans to high-yield borrowers. The loans cover a wide array of industries, with technology being the largest concentration of underlying borrowers.

Matchmaker #3

TRADER (EQUITY, FIXED INCOME AND DERIVATIVES)

Career Path	Undergraduate Degree	Advanced Degree	Personality Type	Level of Teamwork
•MD/Partner •CIO	•Finance •Economics •Math/Statistics	•MBA •CFA •MS in Finance	Extrovert	Medium

Overview

Traders are the ultimate matchmakers. Thousands of times a day they connect buyers with sellers. A trader can be employed on either the sell-side, such as at large banks, or the buy-side, such as mutual funds, hedge funds, and other asset managers discussed earlier.

a) <u>Sell-side Trader</u>: The sell-side trader sits at the trading desks of investment banks and is responsible for establishing the second-by-second market prices. Sell-side traders constantly seek to match buyers and sellers while collecting a spread. For example, a trader that buys Microsoft stock from a buy-side account for $40.25 per share and resells that same stock to another buy-side account for $40.30 per share, collects a $0.05 per share spread (known as a "bid-ask spread"). A sell-side trader can also be known as a "market maker".

b) <u>Buy-side Trader</u>: the primary task of buy-side traders is to get the best price possible for their employer. The buyer at the other end of the previous Microsoft transaction will choose the $40.30 stock over another sell-side trader offering it at $40.31.

There are different traders for different securities and derivatives: equity securities, investment grade bonds, high-yield bonds, futures, options, structured-finance securities, credit-default swaps, currencies, and interest rates, to name just a few.

Trader: What will I do?

- Execute buy and sell orders with the goal of getting the best execution price
- Establish the day-to-day prices of a security based on supply and demand market fundamentals and the financial fundamentals of the underlying security
- Trade stocks, bonds, structured debt, options, and derivatives
- Work with sell-side and buy-side analysts to determine prices, valuations, and trends
- Collaborate as a sell-side trader with colleagues in research (the sell-side analyst) and institutional sales to screen investment ideas and discuss relative value for buy-side investors
- Provide expertise on market dynamics to explain volumes, ownership, buying and selling patterns, and relative value
- Provide expertise on technical issues such as pricing, duration, and spreads

Trader: What skills and qualities help?

- Extremely quick thinker
- Strong math skills
- Tolerant of being tied to a trading desk during market hours
- Willing to be aggressive while searching for the best price
- Accept very little subjectivity in performance reviews which are based largely on profitability

Trader Examples

- Goldman Sachs has four operating divisions. Three of the divisions are i.) Investment Banking, ii.) Investing & Lending (includes Commercial Banking, Private Equity, and Venture Capital), and iii.) Investment Management (includes Asset Management,

Hedge Fund, and Buy-side). The fourth division is Institutional Client Services and is predominantly comprised of trading operations. In a recent three-year period, Goldman generated about $33 billion per year in total revenues, with nearly $15 billion, or 45%, generated through trading. About half of the nearly $15 billion in trading revenues was generated by equities and the rest came through fixed income, commodities, and currencies.

The purpose of including this example was to show the sheer size and variety of trading operations at many of the large investment banks. This book spends a lot of time discussing the non-trading careers such as investment banking, commercial banking, private equity, venture capital, hedge fund, and buy-side. Yet the trading operations alone in this example generates nearly as much as those other businesses combined!

- ABC Bank's trading desk makes markets in computer company Dell's 6% bonds. ABC's traders recently bought the bonds at $87.00 from a pension-fund client and immediately resold them to a hedge-fund client for $87.25, earning a .25 spread.
- Mickey works on the commodity-derivative trading desk at ABC Bank. The bank's client is a large cruise ship company that spends nearly 25% of its expense on fuel. The cruise ship company's treasury team likes to hedge 80% of its 12-month rolling fuel exposure and then hedge 50% of the following 12 months. In effect, it hedges a 24-month period to avoid sharp fuel price increases. Mickey works with his institutional sales colleagues to provide the treasurer current pricing for derivative contracts to lock in the price of fuel for the next two years. Mickey must offset these contracts with other clients who believe future fuel prices are likely to decline.
- XYZ Bank's trading desk specializes in the technology sector. Recently, it has priced bonds for semiconductor-equipment manufacturers Lam Research and KLA-Tencor. The two companies announced a merger to create one of the industry's strongest

companies. To finance the acquisition of KLA-Tencor, Lam issued $2.5 billion in different tranches of senior bonds, including a 4.65% 10-year bond.

A few months after the offering, the 4.65% bonds' value increased to $108 from $100 par in trading. The higher price reduced the bond's yield to less than 4%. The price increase reflected the market's expectation that the combined entity would capture additional market share. Shortly after the increase to $108, the companies announced that the merger's regulatory review would not be completed as quickly as promised. The news prompted investors to worry that the deal would not receive regulatory approval. The legal terms of the 4.65% bonds required Lam to repurchase them at $101 if the merger did not gain approval.

Working with their desk analyst, the traders at XYZ Bank believed the odds of the deal receiving regulatory approval were 50/50. They swiftly adjusted their market price to $104.50 to reflect the risk that the deal would not be approved, in which case the bonds would be worth $101 rather than the $108 value that was anticipated on the strong credit profile of a combined entity.

Matchmaker #3a

INSTITUTIONAL SALES (EQUITY, FIXED INCOME, AND DERIVATIVES)
(Also known as the Sales Desk)

Career Path	Undergraduate Degree	Advanced Degree	Personality Type	Level of Teamwork
MD/Partner	•Finance •Economics •Various other	•MBA •CFA	Extrovert	High

Overview

The institutional-sales specialist role could have been included in either the sell-side trader or the investment banking capital markets sections because this role sits on the trading desk and works closely with those groups. The institutional-sales role, however, skews more toward the relationship side. This person functions as the point person between sell-side analysts, traders, economists, strategists, and investment bankers on one side and buy-side and hedge-fund clients on the other. The primary role is to service those clients and understand their investment mandates. Sales officials ensure clients have access to research, are aware of new bond or equity issuances, and are informed about financial products such as derivatives. They also facilitate trades through traders.

The person holding this role communicates trading inventory to clients explaining what stocks and bonds they can immediately trade in large blocks. They also suggest trade ideas to clients. Like the trader role, there are different institutional sales roles for each type of security: equities, investment-grade fixed income, high-yield fixed income, and derivatives among others.

Institutional Sales: What will I do?

- Have complete understanding of buy-side and hedge fund client mandates, such as limits on the grade of bonds that can be purchased or whether a client precludes investments in companies producing alcohol or tobacco products
- Sit on a trading desk during market hours
- Develop and manage client relationships and accounts
- Work closely with trading and investment banking capital markets colleagues
- Offer trade ideas to buy-side and hedge-fund clients to generate higher trade volumes through the trading desk
- Identify reasons for changes in prices such as specific industry events, macro-economic data, or technical issues, such as supply and demand of a specific security
- Provide market intelligence to clients, such as overall buying and selling patterns
- Commit to usually being at a trading desk during market hours although there is typically more travel than in other roles that strictly require staying at a trading desk
- Introduce clients to subject-matter expert colleagues such as economists and strategists
- Entertain clients at dinners, sporting events, and other outings

Institutional Sales: What skills and qualities help?

- An extroverted personality with strong communication skills
- Enjoy investing, general finance, and financial products
- Strong awareness of current events and of the macro environment
- Problem solving skills that generate creative ideas to benefit your employer and client
- Enjoy the fast pace of capital markets and a trading desk

Institutional Sales Examples

- Sue works in institutional sales on the equity desk of a large global bank. She covers 15 asset manager accounts. She services these accounts by keeping them informed about the latest sell-side research and industry news, and provides access to the banks' team of economists. Additionally, Sue tirelessly keeps track of large holdings and recent buy and sell decisions by her clients. She knows Intel is the largest holding of client ABC Asset Management and that they have actively acquired more shares over the last several months. Sue's sell-side analyst colleague recently wrote a 10-page report on Intel that upgraded the company's stock price target by 25%. Sue immediately sends this report to her client and follows up with a phone call to see if the client wants to speak with the analyst.

- Albert works in institutional sales on the fixed-income desk of the same large global bank. Each morning, he sends five trading ideas to clients that involve swapping bonds with similar risk levels where he believes higher returns can be achieved. These clients only deal in corporate bonds that are rated Baa3/BBB- or higher from the rating agencies and have a duration of ten years or less. Albert makes certain to only send trade ideas that fall within these strict parameters.

- Albert also communicates new bond deals to his buy-side and hedge-fund clients. On a given morning, Albert may communicate four or five new bond deals coming to market where he will list the issuer, their credit ratings, and the Initial Price Talk ("IPT"). The IPT is generated by the investment banking capital markets advisory role and is based on feedback from a roadshow or by comparing the bonds to similar ones being traded. The IPT is a starting point and will ultimately depend on the bonds' supply and demand that Albert tracks.

  For example, Apple could come to the bond market and offer a $1 billion, 10-year bond at an IPT equal to that paid by the

U.S. government's 10-year Treasury plus 120 basis points, known as "T+120". So if the 10-year Treasury (which is considered extremely safe) was 2.50%, then the yield for Apple's bond would start at 3.70%. However, let's assume that the Apple bond is very popular with investors so there are $5 billion in orders for the $1 billion offer. In that case, Albert works with his investment banking capital markets colleagues to revise the pricing and communicate that change to clients. It may move down to T+90 for a 3.40% yield. More adjustments up or down may be required to secure the best pricing for Apple while generating $1 billion in orders.

- Andrew works in institutional sales for ABC Bank, a global institution that lends money and advises companies. Andrew specializes in interest rate-related derivatives. He regularly meets with his commercial-banking colleague Jeff to learn about clients that have committed lines of credit and bank loans from ABC. Andrew briefs the chief financial officers (CFO) and treasurers of those clients on interest rate expectations and presents a slide deck detailing treasury curves (the direction interest rates are expected to go). He recently met with the CFO and treasurer of Generic Pharmaceutical to present a slide deck detailing the company's existing capital structure of fixed-coupon debt. He showed that they could swap some to floating-rate obligations using derivative contracts. He also presented details of a treasury-lock contract to lock in the treasury rate for a bond deal they expect to issue six months in the future. The goal is to generate business while improving the client's financial picture.

Matchmaker #4:

INVESTOR BUSINESS DEVELOPMENT
(Also known as Investor Marketing)

Career Path	Undergraduate Degree	Advanced Degree	Personality Type	Level of Teamwork
MD/Partner	•Finance •Economics •Marketing •Various other	•MBA •CFA	Extrovert	Medium

Overview

The investor business-development career is vast and features various roles focused on matching asset owners and investors with asset managers. For the purposes of this book, think of this role in the following two separate specializations:

a) <u>Capital-Raising Business Development</u>: This role focuses on raising funds for asset managers, venture-capital funds, private-equity funds, middle-market lenders, and hedge funds. This individual prospects high-net-worth individuals, corporations, pension funds, insurance companies, third-party managers, and governments to encourage them to steer investment to their funds. This role typically tries to persuade customers using historical performance, strategies, investor biographies, and competitive advantages of their funds.

b) <u>Financial Product Wholesaler</u>: This position focuses on people who sell financial products such as mutual funds and ETF's to a 401(k) plan or wealth manager.

Investor Business Development: What will I do?

- Prospect new clients to invest in your funds
- Function as the point of contact for investors

- Develop a command of product, services, pricing, advantages, and competitors
- Communicate overall market trends and value proposition
- Attend industry conferences and trade shows

Investor Business Development: What skills and qualities help?

- Sales mentality
- An extroverted personality
- Strong communication, presentation, and sales skills
- Enjoy investments, general finance, and financial products
- Enjoy current events and developing a broad understanding of the macro business environment

Investor Business Development Examples

- Kelly is a wholesaler for ABC mutual funds. ABC has 50 mutual funds that span investing priorities such as income, growth, and emerging markets. Kelly is responsible for prospecting corporate 401(k) managers and wealth managers to include ABC's funds in their offerings. She pitches ABC's historical performance, ratings, and portfolio-manager biographies with prospective clients.
- Mike works in business development for XYZ Asset Management. XYZ specializes in short-duration corporate bonds, investing only in securities with a maximum maturity of two years. XYZ has a team of 12 buy-side research analysts who have an MBA degree and a CFA charter. XYZ has a five-year streak of beating the primary benchmarks for a similar short-duration strategy. Mike is prospecting ABC Sovereign Wealth Fund, hoping it will invest at least $100 million with XYZ. Mike uses a 15-page slide deck detailing XYZ's historic performance and the biographies of its credit research team.
- Merly works in business development for private equity firm ABC Capital. ABC has $5 billion under management that can be

invested in 10 different businesses at any one time. ABC acquires companies in hopes of improving operations and financial performance before re-selling them to a larger corporation or doing an initial public offering. ABC has no intention of selling any of its existing 10 companies right now. But the firm would like to raise another $1 billion to continue acquiring companies. Merly is prospecting third-party managers around the country that represent state pension funds and university endowments. Her hope is to raise the $1 billion from these asset owners by showing them ABC's strong track record of performance generated by a richly experienced management team.

- Kenny works for middle-market lending company MM Capital. His job is to prospect outside investors to invest in the company's loans. In this role, Kenny travels around the country meeting with pension funds, insurance companies, sovereign-wealth funds, university endowments, and the treasury departments of large corporations. These entities are key prospects since they manage a lot of money but do not have the infrastructure to reach small borrowers spread across the country. MM Capital captures a spread between the interest they charge to borrowers and the rate they pay to investors. It also charges a smaller management fee than many competitors. Kenny uses the opportunity to pitch quality loans with relatively low fees to investors.

PART III

NEXT STEPS AND FINAL THOUGHTS

I wrote this book to provide a bird's-eye view of more than 30 career paths possible with a business degree. I hope you appreciate the wide variety of careers and begin to understand the qualifications those paths require and where your personality may fit.

You may have found some careers you want to investigate further. If this book convinced you not to study business at all, I hope you find a career to suit your passion. Perhaps some of the science careers discussed in the product-development section sound more compelling!

If you did find business careers that piqued your interest, consider this the first step toward a long and fulfilling career. To move forward on your career journey, follow these tips:

1) **<u>Get Good Grades</u>**: I cannot emphasize enough the importance of having an impressive academic record. Strong grades put you in the driver's seat for the career you want.
2) **<u>Do Deeper Research</u>**: The "syllabus test" I mentioned in the introduction is designed to make you think which of the 32 careers you want to learn more about. The career pages introduce some broad themes, key terms, and typical scenarios to pique your interest. Use that framework to launch deeper research. Search job openings and look at key requirements listed. Search company annual reports, websites, and investor-day presentations for

companies in the fields you like. Begin reading business-related magazines, websites, and newspapers to get fluent on major business topics and the lingo that typically accompanies those careers.

3) **Speak with Working Adults**: Some people just beginning a career search are reluctant to approach older people for advice and suggestions. Please don't be! Most people are happy to talk about their experiences. They were in your shoes once and recognize that finding a suitable career is important. Reach out to people to discover what they like and dislike about their careers. Ask what they would repeat and what they may have done differently if they could do it again. You might even ask about some job shadowing opportunities.

4) **Look Ahead**: Investing some time thinking about where you want to be 20 to 30 years from now goes a long way in getting on the right career path. If you shudder at the prospect of traveling or of managing large teams, the careers on the chief executive officer path might not be for you. Think about the examples of an individual who was a general manager in Europe or Asia before becoming chief executive officer. If that relocation-heavy lifestyle excites you then it might be a path to follow. Alternatively, if investing other people's money would prevent you from getting a decent night's sleep, careers on the chief investment officer path are probably best avoided.

5) **Work with Your Career Center**: Hopefully you read this while attending or considering a school that has a business program and an accompanying career center. Visit those centers to learn about internship and placement opportunities. If you are intrigued by a specific industry or career, ask what types of companies recruit at your school. Make your ambitions clear to your counselors and take advantage of the resources they offer. If the school does not have a direct connection with the kinds of companies you are interested in, ask the career professionals to help you to create those links. Just because a company does not recruit at your school does not mean you can't earn an internship or job. You may have to show more initiative and effort but that will be recognized by your target employer.

Use these five strategies to build on what you've learned in these pages as you start your career journey. As you navigate that path, be mindful of where you are, where you are going, what you hope to achieve, and how you plan to make that happen.

Great careers are possible but they usually don't happen by accident. You've shown true initiative by using this book to get started in your search. Continuing this proactive approach will pave the way to a rewarding future. Good luck and enjoy your journey!

83155561R00115

Made in the USA
Middletown, DE
09 August 2018